The Healthy Mac
Preventive Care, Practical Diagnostics, and Proven Remedies

Heather Morris
Joli Ballew

Mc
Graw
Hill

New York Chicago San Francisco Lisbon
London Madrid Mexico City Milan New Delhi
San Juan Seoul Singapore Sydney Toronto

The McGraw·Hill Companies

Cataloging-in-Publication Data is on file with the Library of Congress

McGraw-Hill books are available at special quantity discounts to use as premiums and sales promotions, or for use in corporate training programs. To contact a representative, please e-mail us at bulksales@mcgraw-hill.com.

The Healthy Mac: Preventive Care, Practical Diagnostics, and Proven Remedies

1234567890   QFR QFR   1098765432

ISBN   978-0-07-179834-1
MHID   0-07-179834-X

Sponsoring Editor Roger Stewart	**Technical Editor** Guy Hart-Davis	**Composition** Cenveo Publisher Services
Editorial Supervisor Janet Walden	**Copy Editor** Margaret Berson	**Illustration** Cenveo Publisher Services
Project Manager Harleen Chopra, Cenveo Publisher Services	**Proofreader** Susie Elkind	**Art Director, Cover** Jeff Weeks
Acquisitions Coordinator Ryan Willard	**Indexer** Jack Lewis	**Cover Designer** Mary McKeon
	Production Supervisor James Kussow	

For Dave
—HM

About the Authors

Heather Morris is a technical writer and editor with more than eight years experience in publishing. She is the author of easy-to-use technology guides, including *Researching Your Family History Online*, *Scanning and Editing Your Old Photographs*, *Starting Up an Online Business*, and *Pinterest Kickstart*. A lifelong Apple enthusiast, she currently lives in a technology-infused household in the San Francisco Bay Area with her husband, two sons, and a half dozen or more iOS devices and computers.

Joli Ballew is a technical writer, college professor, operating system expert, and gadget enthusiast. She's written over 50 books on topics ranging from operating systems to smartphones to tablets to photo editing programs. Some of her books include *How to Do Everything: iPad, Third Edition; Operating Systems Demystified; How to Do Everything: Netbooks;* and *Kindle Fire QuickSteps*, all with McGraw-Hill.

About the Technical Editor

Guy Hart-Davis is the author of more than 80 computer books, including *The Healthy PC, iPad Geekery, iPhone 4S Geekery, Kindle Fire Geekery,* and *iMac Portable Genius, Fourth Edition.*

Contents

x Contents

Acknowledgments

The authors would like to thank the following people for their help creating this book:

- Roger Stewart, Ryan Willard, and Janet Walden at McGraw-Hill for their ongoing support through each stage of writing and production.
- Guy Hart-Davis for his helpful feedback and encouragement.
- Margaret Berson for carefully reviewing the manuscript.
- Harleen Chopra at Cenveo for coordinating the production of the book.
- Susie Elkind for proofreading the pages.
- Jack Lewis for creating the index.

And the authors also thank their agent, Neil Salkind, Ph.D., of the Salkind Literary Agency.

Introduction

Macs have a reputation as being easy to use and reliable, but even the newest models can succumb to data loss, buggy applications, malware, networking issues, and more. This book shows you, step by step, how to maintain and protect your data, make the most of essential applications and features, keep your computer safe, protect yourself online and over a network, and improve your Mac's performance.

This book is for anyone who wants to keep their Mac running at peak condition by learning how to maintain data, optimize applications, and enable security settings, as well as troubleshoot problems when they arise.

We use Mountain Lion OS X throughout the book, but the advice can apply to any version of OS X, with a few tweaks. Differences between Mountain Lion and Snow Leopard and Lion are noted throughout.

You can work through each chapter in order or skip ahead to a chapter to help you solve a particular problem straight away.

How Is This Book Organized?

In Part I of this book, you'll learn how to improve your Mac's performance and optimize the data on your computer.

Chapter 1 helps you identify problems and review the technical specifications of your Mac. With those details in hand, you learn how to perform essential fixes including adding RAM, addressing disk space issues, and upgrading to the most recent OS X.

Chapter 2 shows you how to optimize the data on your Mac and free up more disk space by removing content that you don't need. Once you've decluttered your computer, you learn how to make the most of the data you want to keep by creating a filing system that works for you.

Chapter 3 explains how to get rid of applications you don't use as well as all the related files that can gunk up your Mac. You also learn how to scan for and remove viruses and other types of malware to keep your computer healthy.

Chapter 4 helps you customize OS X and make it work the way you want. We show you how to configure the desktop, Notifications, the Dock, Mission Control, and more.

Part II covers the essential applications and features of OS X and helps you make the most of each.

Chapter 5 walks you through how to optimize iTunes and manage all the media files in your library. You learn how to get rid of duplicate or unwanted data, configure file types to save space, make the most of your syncing options, and share your media over a network.

Chapter 6 shows you how to make the most of Mail on your Mac. You learn how to take advantage of Mail's features to reduce spam, manage junk mail, and organize the mail you want to keep.

Chapter 7 explains how to get the most out of your browsing with Safari, manage bookmarks and tabs, and make use of features like Private Browsing and Reader. We also show you how to maximize the security of your personal information while online.

Chapter 8 helps you make the most of Mountain Lion's new features like expanded iCloud functions, AutoSave, and Versions. You also learn how to control features you might not enjoy, like "natural scrolling" and Resume.

Part III helps you make the most of your network, securing your Mac, and resolving problems when they occur by learning basic troubleshooting tasks.

Chapter 9 shows you how to protect your privacy and your personal information by enabling many of the built-in security features that come with OS X. We walk you through setting up individual user accounts, enabling the Firewall and FileVault, and disabling automatic login.

Chapter 10 walks you through setting up a secure network, whether wireless or Ethernet. You learn how to share data safely between Macs on your network.

Chapter 11 focuses on how to set up a secure network between Macs and Windows PCs. We show you how to enable safe sharing options on both your Windows PC and Mac. If you have problems setting up connections between the two, you'll learn how to resolve some of the common problems that crop up.

Chapter 12 helps you identify some of the problems that can slow down booting and the overall performance of your Mac. We show you how to monitor your Mac's performance by running performance tests and making use of the Activity Monitor, as well as how to make a number of small changes that will revive a sluggish computer.

Chapter 13 shows you how to increase the security of your Mac by enhancing physical security and enabling advanced security options. You also learn about the keychain and how to create safe passwords to protect your privacy and personal information.

Chapter 14 outlines several troubleshooting steps you can take to resolve problems on your Mac as they occur. We show you how to deal with buggy or unresponsive applications, repair your hard disk if needed, and even reinstall OS X when appropriate.

1 Identify Problems and Boost Performance

A healthy Mac should perform all of the tasks that you want it to, quickly and easily. In this chapter you'll learn to identify some of the problems associated with an unhealthy computer, learn about the specifics of your Mac, and try some essential fixes including updating your operating system, fixing disk space issues, and adding more memory if you need to.

Note In the first chapter you will see some screen shots from a pre–Mountain Lion Mac. We suggest you upgrade to Mountain Lion if you aren't using it already. The rest of the book will be written with Mountain Lion in mind, although the techniques can be applied to any Apple OS with a little tweaking.

Identify Problems

There are a number of potential problems that can cause your Mac to lose its former speed and efficiency: you may be low on disk space, have piles of unwanted data, or maybe you inadvertently downloaded some malware. There are more issues than are listed here, but as you read through this section, you can start to see where some of the problems arise.

Your Mac Has Slowed Down and Takes a Long Time to Start Up

All Macs slow down a little over time, but you should be able to accomplish most of your daily tasks without the constant presence of the "spinning beach ball of doom."

If you find you have lots of time on your hands waiting for your Mac to start up, or you are waiting for it to do more than two things at once, these are symptoms that you should pay attention to. Even if you've had a Mac for a few years, you should be able to start up quickly and have all of your favorite applications open at the same time. There are several remedies to revive a sluggish computer that we'll explore throughout the book (if you want to get started now, go to the section "Boost Your Mac's Performance" near the end of this chapter).

You Don't Regularly Update Your Apps and OS X

Keeping your applications and OS X up to date is essential in preventing problems from occurring on your Mac in the first place. If you regularly ignore Software Update and don't take advantage of updates to or new versions of OS X, then you aren't taking advantage of bug fixes, security updates, and other improvements that keep your Mac healthy. Keeping up with updates will not only solve many common problems like crashes and slowdowns; in many cases, it will prevent them from happening in the first place. In this chapter, we'll show you how to check for updates as well as how to upgrade to the most recent OS X.

You Have Too Many Installed Programs

You may have programs lingering on your hard drive that you no longer use or perhaps forgot about. Those unwanted programs can take up lots of disk space that can slow you down and could be better devoted to other resources. They might even be configured to start when your Mac does and run in the background. Third-party applications are also notorious sources of bugs and worse. Sometimes, getting rid of such apps will rid your Mac of troublesome quirks. You can find information about uninstalling these items in Chapter 3.

You Have Unwanted Installation Files, Downloads, and Lots of Disorganized Files

Data you create can clog up your Mac, but there is also lots of data that finds its way to your computer when you install new programs, update old ones, and download information from email or the Internet. Like an unwelcome houseguest, they show up without an invitation and start taking up needed resources. In order to show them the door, you'll need to identify them—Chapter 3 will show you how.

You Don't Have a Backup Strategy You Trust

You've no doubt been admonished time and again to back up the contents of your Mac, and not without good reason. No operating system is completely immune to failed hard drives, and accidentally deleting data is a common mishap for even the most experienced users. To preserve important data like work files or valued family photographs and movies, take advantage of Apple's built-in backup application. Not only does it preserve essential files, but you can use Time Machine to restore your

Mac if your hard drive becomes corrupted or damaged. See the sidebar "Back Up to Time Machine" later in this chapter for how to set up regular backups.

Your Desktop, Dock, Finder, Launchpad, and Mission Control Are Overrun

Clutter slows you down. At work, looking for a file in a big pile of papers is time-consuming. At home, looking for a paper clip in a drawer full of junk does likewise. Similarly, if you have clutter on the Desktop, Dock, Finder, and so on, it will make what you want to find every so often difficult to get to. If you spend a lot of time looking for stuff, consider tidying up. Chapter 2 has ideas for how to do this and includes tips on making the most of the existing file system on your Mac, and Chapter 4 will help you make the most of essential features of OS X like Launchpad and Mission Control.

You Get Junk Email and Have No Strategy in Place for Organizing What You Want to Keep

In addition to being a major annoyance, junk mail can contain malicious items like malware. Furthermore, lots of unwanted items in your Mail can clog up your Mac and make it difficult to find what you want. We'll show you how to keep tabs on spam, manage the mail you want to keep, and make the most of Apple's Mail application in Chapter 6.

You Don't Know How to Make Use of Newer OS X Features

You scroll up, and the screen goes down! You swipe sideways with three fingers and the whole window seems to move off the desktop! If you haven't had experience with one of the many iOS devices offered by Apple, then the changed style of interaction with your Mac in Mountain Lion may be very frustrating indeed, and even interfere with your use of the computer. While this new way of working with your Mac may present new challenges, the new OS Xes have a lot to offer; we'll explore some of these features and help you tame your cat in Chapter 8.

People Can Access Your Computer When You're Away from It

Another potential risk to the health of your Mac is the possibility of someone else accessing it while you are away and, intentionally or not, causing harm to your files or computer. There are a number of basic security steps you can take to ensure that your privacy and personal information are protected. At a minimum, you should make use of the built-in security settings in OS X and create user accounts for everyone who uses the Mac. There are many more steps you can take as well, which we'll explore in Chapters 9 and 13.

Learn About Multi-Touch Gestures

One feature of the newer operating systems is the prominence of Multi-Touch gestures. We are not referring to the more colorful gestures you might be disposed to make when your Mac is not behaving as you want. Rather, you perform gestures on your trackpad or Magic Mouse to control what you see on your screen. The functions of most gestures can also be accomplished with keyboard shortcuts and contextual menus. Do give the Multi-Touch gestures a try as you might grow to like them.

Some common gestures:

- **Two-finger scroll**   To scroll through documents and web sites, slide two fingers up and down on your trackpad.
- **Pinch to zoom**   Pinch your thumb and finger together and apart to zoom in and out of web pages and images.
- **Tap to click**   Tap once to click or twice to double-click with one finger on your trackpad.
- **Rotate**   With your thumb and finger, twist clockwise or counterclockwise to rotate an image.

You Can't Connect to Networked Computers or Shared Resources or They Can't Connect to You

If you have more than one computer in your home, Apple makes it relatively simple to network them with a Wi-Fi or an Ethernet connection. You can connect a Mac to a Mac and also share files between your Mac and PC. However, sometimes these connections fail or you can only share data one way. See Chapters 10 and 11 for information on how to manage your networks and share data safely between computers.

Malware Is a New Threat and You Aren't Sure About Cookies

Security threats to your Mac, including malware and phishing scams, are increasing. You can also inadvertently get malware when you download what you think is a benign file from somewhere on the Web (these hidden programs are called Trojan horses). In addition to these invasive threats, you are constantly leaving little trails of information about yourself (cookies) on web sites you visit and when you do things like fill in and submit forms, access account numbers, or use the Auto Fill feature in your web browser. We look at several strategies for addressing these problems in Chapters 3, 6, and 13.

Know Your Mac

Whether you have a MacBook, iMac, Mac mini, or something else, your computer has its own unique set of specifications. Specifications include things like the type of model you have, the operating system, hard drive space, and amount of RAM (memory), among others. Knowledge of these details helps you look after your Mac properly and do things like update your software or hardware if needed. In addition, should you ever need to talk to a computer repair person on the phone, you can be sure that one of the first questions they'll ask is about the specs and OS version.

Find Your Model and OS

Before you start to work through the steps and suggestions in this book, you need to know the specifics of your model and OS X. While the most fervent Mac users may be able to rattle these details off the top of their heads, the rest of us will probably need to look them up. Even if you don't write down the details now, you'll need to remember where to find this information when you make needed upgrades to your computer. File these steps away for future reference or when you upgrade your operating system in the next section.

To find out about your operating system and processor, do the following as shown here on a Mac running Mountain Lion:

1. Go to the Apple menu and select About This Mac, and then click More Info.

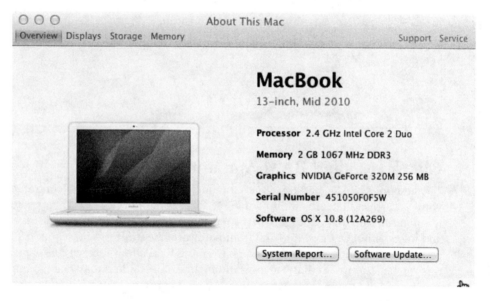

2. Write down the model name and information (for example, MacBook 13-inch, Mid 2010).
3. Look for the OS X version information (Version 10.7, Version 10.8).
4. Note the type of processor (Intel Core 2 Duo, Core i5 or i7, or Xeon processor, and so on).

To find the same details on an earlier operating system, go to the Apple menu and select About This Mac and click More Info. Select Hardware and look for the Model Name and other information, as shown here.

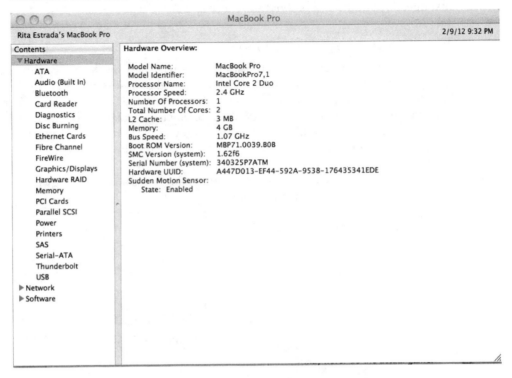

Check Installed RAM Amount and Type

The amount of RAM (random access memory) your Mac has plays a central role in your Mac's overall health and functioning. RAM is memory that your computer uses to temporarily store data from an open application, commands it believes it may need later, and information being sent to and from hardware like printers and scanners. If your computer is slowing down when you have more than a few applications open at once, this can be a symptom that you are running low on RAM and may need to upgrade.

To find out about your Mac's memory on a computer running Snow Leopard, do the following:

1. Select About This Mac from the Apple menu and click More Info.
2. Click Memory and note the number and type of memory cards (see Figure 1-1).

To find out about the amount of RAM on a computer running Lion or Mountain Lion, do the following:

1. Select About This Mac from the menu and click More Info.
2. Click the Memory tab at the top of the window and note the number of memory slots and the type of memory your Mac accepts (see Figure 1-2).

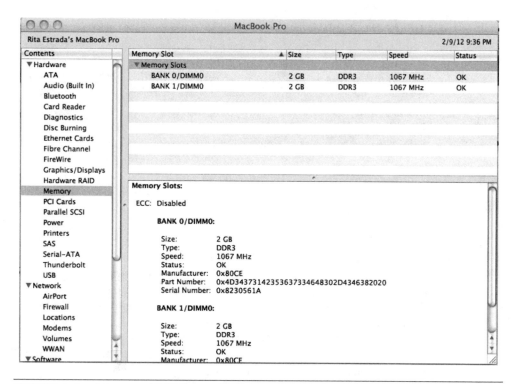

FIGURE 1-1   Memory (RAM) installed on a MacBook Pro running Snow Leopard

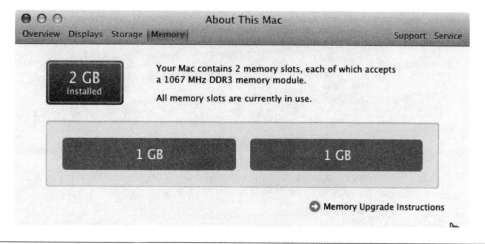

FIGURE 1-2   Memory slots and type on a MacBook running Mountain Lion

Check Disk Space

Disk space refers to the amount of space on your Mac's hard drive, where your operating system, applications, documents, music, and other files are stored. To check on your disk space on a computer running Mountain Lion, do the following:

1. Select About This Mac from the Apple menu.
2. Click More Info.
3. Click Storage to see how much of your hard drive is used (see Figure 1-3).

Note
To check disk space on a Mac running an earlier OS X, select About This Mac from the Apple menu and click More Info. Select Storage from the window's sidebar to view disk space.

There is no hard and fast rule about how much disk space you need to keep free. How much you need depends on how you use your Mac and how it is currently functioning. If you frequently use video, photo, or audio applications, you want to leave more disk space free. These applications need some of the disk space for virtual memory. Generally speaking, it is a good idea to keep at least 15 percent of your hard drive free. You can have less, but you need to assess how your Mac is currently functioning and whether you have slow periods when working with certain applications or if your computer has slowed down a lot recently—or you may have even seen a dialog box pop up warning you that space is low.

Note
We refer to your disk or hard disk throughout the book, though your Mac may have more than one disk or you may have a high-performance SSD (solid-state drive).

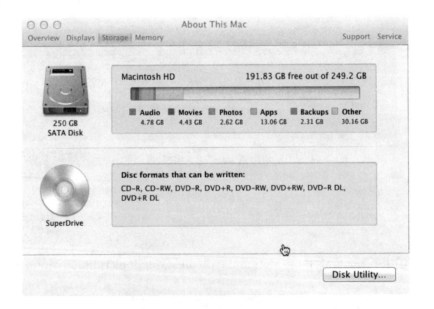

FIGURE 1-3   Determine how much hard disk space is being used.

Look For and Install Available Updates

Apple and other developers regularly update their software to fix minor bugs or to fine-tune and improve the functioning of the programs, including adding important security fixes. Get in the habit of checking for and installing updates as a first step in keeping your Mac healthy. Updates differ depending on the operating system you are running. In Mountain Lion, you are taken to the App Store for updates, while Snow Leopard and Lion have their own Software Update window that you work with. You need to be connected to the Internet to perform the following tasks.

To check for updates in Mountain Lion:

1. From the Apple menu, select Software Update. You'll be taken to the App Store and see a screen like the one in Figure 1-4. If there aren't any available updates, you'll see "No Updates Available" in the App Store window.
2. Review the list of updates and click More to see what the updates contain. Occasionally, the update won't apply to you because it's for a piece of hardware you don't have, or software you no longer use. You can skip those updates, but you should always upgrade any new offerings for OS X and applications that come with your Mac.
3. Click the Update button next to the software you want to update. A status bar will display showing the estimated amount of time to complete the update.
4. Quit the App Store when your software is finished updating. If a restart is required to complete the update, you'll be prompted to restart your Mac.

FIGURE 1-4   Software updates are done through the App Store in Mountain Lion.

To check for updates in Lion or an earlier OS X:

1. Select Software Update from the Apple menu. A window will appear with the message "checking for new software." After a short wait, you will get a new window saying either that your software is up to date or that there are available updates.
2. Click Continue to view the updates. You select which updates to apply. For example, you may not want certain updates for hardware or software you no longer use. If the item has a small triangle icon next to it, your Mac will be restarted after it's installed. If you don't have time to update your software then and there, you can come back and do it when you have a few minutes to perform the update and restart your Mac if needed.

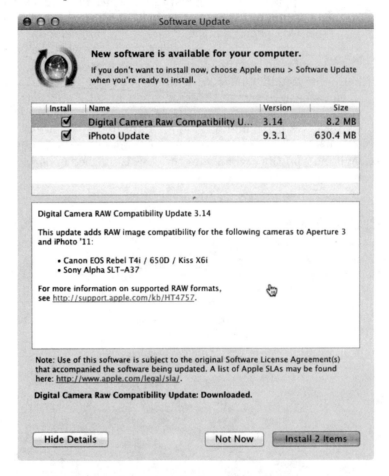

3. Click the Install button when you are ready to install the update.

In Mountain Lion, your Mac is set to check for updates automatically by default. There is also a new option enabled that will download newly available updates in the background, and install system data files and security updates when they're available. This behind-the-scenes update process is there to keep your computer free from bugs and malware, and to optimize your applications. The updates won't install automatically—you'll know when they are available when you see a notification banner alerting you.

In addition to Apple applications and those you purchased in the App Store, you'll need to keep any third-party applications up to date as well. Some will alert you when there are available updates, while others you'll need to check for manually. Many applications have a Check for Updates command in their menu. If you don't see an update feature within the application, you can check on the developer's web site for the most recent upgrades.

Boost Your Mac's Performance

In this next section we'll outline three remedies you can apply to boost your ailing Mac and prevent problems, including: adding RAM, fixing disk space issues, and upgrading your OS X. You may not need to try all of the remedies outlined here right away. For example, you might have heaps of disk space and have a RAM amount that is currently working fine for your purposes. However, we will strongly encourage you to update OS X whenever possible to keep your Mac performing at its best and keep you protected from new bugs and security problems.

Add RAM If Your Mac Is Short

Having sufficient RAM is vital to the health of your Mac and it is one of the biggest factors in how quickly your applications open, how easily you can switch between them, and how many you can run at once. If the amount of RAM available on your Mac is less than the amount needed to support open applications, your computer can hang up, crash, or otherwise cause you grief.

How much RAM to add depends in part on how much RAM your Mac currently has, and how much your computer can hold. If your Mac can only hold up to 8GB of RAM, for example, then that is the maximum you can have. Review your Mac's RAM capabilities by following the instructions in the section "Check Installed RAM Amount and Type" earlier in this chapter. If possible, install the maximum amount your Mac can hold, or anywhere from 8GB to 16GB. Even an increase from 2GB to 4GB will provide you with a noticeable boost in performance. Apple recommends that you install a module in each memory slot that are the same size. So, if you currently have two memory slots with 1GB each and can go up to 4GB, you'll need to install two more 1GB modules in each slot to achieve the best results.

You can buy RAM from the online Apple store or from a reputable online retailer. RAM purchased directly from Apple is more expensive, but you can be certain that the memory cards are the correct type for your Mac model. If you buy from elsewhere, double-check with the vendor that the RAM is compatible with your model and operating system.

Tip   If you need more help finding compatible RAM for your Mac, you can use free online scanners to help figure it out. One such tool is Crucial Mac Scanner. Go to www.crucial.com/store/drammemory.aspx and click the Scan My System button. You download a small application and run it to find the exact RAM type needed, how much you can add, and how many memory slots you have.

Installing RAM on your Mac may seem like a daunting task, but there is more than one way to go about it. By far the quickest approach is to install it yourself. On most models, this entails removing a few screws and inserting the additional RAM modules. To install RAM yourself, you need to find the instructions for your Mac model, which can be found by doing the following in Lion or Mountain Lion:

1. Select About This Mac from the Apple menu.
2. Click More Info, and then click the Memory tab.
3. Click Memory Upgrade Instructions (you'll be taken to the Apple web site).
4. Select your Mac model in the list by clicking its link in the list.
5. Review the memory specifications and instructions for how to install RAM on your particular Mac.

You can also look through the paperwork that came with your Mac when you first bought it. There should be a booklet or a set of papers that includes steps and illustrations for adding RAM to your specific Mac model.

If you'd prefer not to do it yourself, you can have the RAM that you purchased on the Apple web site installed for you at an Apple retail store. You'll need to make an appointment online or call for an appointment to get this done.

Tip   If you want to defer buying and installing new RAM but still need a quick boost, you should keep track of, and reduce, the number of windows, applications, and tabs you have open at any one time. Even idle programs that you've opened but aren't currently using will gobble up RAM.

Fix Disk Space Issues If You Have Them

If you find that your Macintosh HD has little room to spare or if you've received a warning message, you have issues with disk space that need to be remedied. We'll show you ways to reduce waste on your disk throughout the book, but if your hard drive is close to full now, then you should take steps sooner.

The easiest way to free up disk space is to either delete or move very large files from your Mac. Rather than going through each of your folders, you can use one of several free utilities that show you how your hard drive is being used. Some useful free utilities are Disk Inventory X and GrandPerspective—both developed specifically to scan OS X. Each scans your disk and graphically displays the size of files.

To assess the size of files taking up space with GrandPerspective:

1. Launch GrandPerspective and select Macintosh HD in the sidebar, and then click Scan. When the scan is complete, you'll see a window similar to the one in Figure 1-5. Each rectangle on the grid represents a file on your Mac. The larger the rectangle, the bigger the file. If a file is part of a folder, you'll see a thin white line around the group when you point your cursor at it.
2. Point your cursor at one of the large rectangles to see what the file is. You'll see the file path at the bottom of the window and also the size of the file.

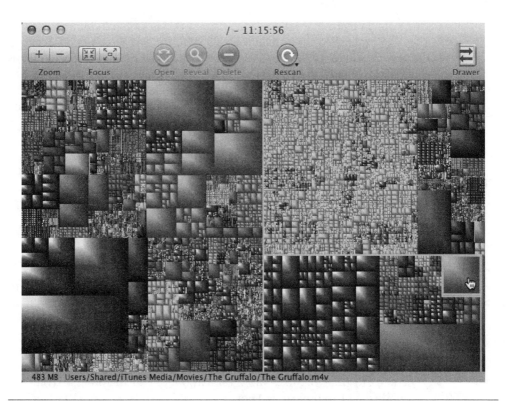

FIGURE 1-5 Each rectangle in GrandPerspective represents a file on your Mac.

3. Click the file and then click Reveal at the top of the window to view the item in a Finder window. You can take a closer look at the file in the Finder window and decide whether to delete it if you no longer need it, or to move it to another location like an external hard drive or optical disc.

Note If you want to delete the file while you are in the application, you have to enable this option. Click the GrandPerspective menu and select Preferences. Next to Enable deletion of, select Files from the pop-up menu. Leave the check box next to Always require confirmation selected.

If you prefer not to use a utility to identify or delete large unneeded files, you can look at some common places where larger files are likely to hide. For more information on this, see the section "Delete Data You Don't Need" in Chapter 2.

Update Your Operating System

Mountain Lion was released in July 2012. If you bought a computer in late 2012, you may have Mountain Lion installed. If you don't have the most recent OS X, you'll need to update your Mac to make the most of this book.

One notable feature of recent operating systems (Lion and Mountain Lion) is that they are available to download through the App Store. You don't have to buy installation discs and install the OS yourself; the whole upgrade process can be accomplished with a few clicks in the App Store. If you have more than one Mac, you can download the operating system to all your computers after the initial purchase. Mountain Lion functions more like iOS, the operating system on your iPhone and iPad, and incorporates many of the gestures used in iOS including the zoom, natural scrolling, and taps on your trackpad or Magic Mouse.

Caution Some older types of third-party software, including Quicken 2007, aren't supported in Mountain Lion. If you have a favorite, third-party program that you rely on, check with the developer before you upgrade to see whether it will be supported in Mountain Lion.

Perform Checks Before You Upgrade

There are a few requirements that your Mac needs to meet before you can upgrade to Mountain Lion. The technical specifications are included here, but you'll also need to make sure that you have enough free disk space and have a recent backup of your hard disk—among other things. Before you upgrade to Mountain Lion:

1. Confirm that you are running Snow Leopard 10.6.8 or the most recent Lion OS X. You can't upgrade to Mountain Lion without one or the other. If you need to upgrade, you can buy Snow Leopard from the Apple store online, install it, and then upgrade directly to Mountain Lion.
2. Confirm that you have one of the following models of Mac: iMac (Mid 2007 or newer), MacBook (Late 2008 Aluminum, or Early 2009 or newer), MacBook Pro (Mid/Late 2007 or newer), MacBook Air (Late 2008 or newer), Mac mini (Early 2009 or newer), or Mac Pro (Early 2008 or newer) Xserve (Early 2009).
3. Perform a Software Update to ensure you have the latest version of the OS X you are currently running.
4. Back up your Mac. See the upcoming sidebar "Back Up to Time Machine" for help.
5. Check whether you have enough free disk space. Apple recommends at least 4GB of free space.

Note Apple states that your Mac only needs 2GB of RAM to install and run Mountain Lion. However, if you are running low on memory or regularly use very graphics-heavy programs, you may find that your computer will run more slowly with Mountain Lion. If you find this to be the case, you can add more RAM. See the section "Add Ram If Your Mac Is Short" earlier in the chapter.

Back Up to Time Machine

If you rarely perform a backup of your Mac, or worse, have never done a backup, take advantage of OS X's built-in backup application, Time Machine. Once you set it up, which takes just a few minutes, it automatically backs up your whole system including document files, system files, programs, music, photos, and more. Throughout this book we'll encourage you (again and again!) to back up prior to performing many of the suggested tasks.

After the first backup, Time Machine checks for changes to files and settings on your Mac each hour, and then backs up those changes. It also keeps daily backups for a month and weekly backups for previous months. These snapshots of your Mac can help you find a file at any given point in time. For example, if you inadvertently delete valued photos, you can go to the backup that last contained those photos (whenever that was) and restore them with Time Machine.

While backing up with Time Machine is incredibly simple, you need something to back up *to*. Because of the volume of content that Time Machine backs up, you need an external hard drive or Apple's Time Capsule—it can't be accomplished with optical drives (CDs and DVDs).

To enable Time Machine, do the following:

1. Plug the external drive into your Mac. A window will appear as shown here asking if you want to use the drive as a backup disk.

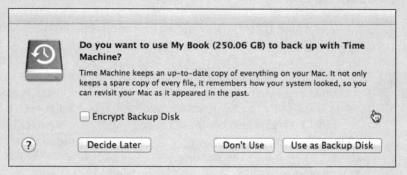

> **Do you want to use My Book (250.06 GB) to back up with Time Machine?**
>
> Time Machine keeps an up-to-date copy of everything on your Mac. It not only keeps a spare copy of every file, it remembers how your system looked, so you can revisit your Mac as it appeared in the past.
>
> ☐ Encrypt Backup Disk
>
> (?)   [Decide Later]   [Don't Use]   [Use as Backup Disk]

2. Click Use as Backup Disk.

The first time you set up Time Machine, it will do an initial backup of your entire system, which can take several hours. Leave your Mac on and don't interrupt or stop the backup. After the first backup is complete, Time Machine will back up changes every hour until your external drive is full. Once the drive is full, your system will begin deleting the oldest files first to make room for new backups.

Install the Latest OS X

Once you have a backup in place and some spare time, you are ready to upgrade to the latest operating system through Apple's App Store. Because it is a download over the Internet, you should be prepared for it to take at least an hour and more likely several, depending on your connection. Despite the time involved, Apple has made this OS X upgrade an absolute breeze to perform. To upgrade to Mountain Lion, do the following as shown here:

1. Open the App Store from your Dock.
2. Click OS X Mountain Lion.
3. Click the Download button, and then click Buy App when it appears.

OS X Mountain Lion

The world's most advanced desktop operating system gets even better.

Download ▾

OS X Mountain Lion

4. Enter your Apple ID and password when prompted and Mountain Lion will start to download.

Tip   If you have more than one Mac, your initial purchase entitles you to install Mountain Lion on your other computers as well. You can install it again through the App Store, but a quicker approach is to copy the installer onto a flash drive, external hard drive, or DVD and install it on your other computers that way (rather than waiting another hour or more for the installer to download on an additional Mac). You have to copy the installer *before* you start it on the first Mac. Once Mountain Lion is installed, it automatically deletes the installer.

5. Once you see the Mountain Lion installer, double-click Install OS X Mountain Lion application.
6. Click Continue and click Agree to the software and license agreement.
7. Click Install and provide your admin user name and password when prompted.

Installation can take a half an hour or more, depending on your Mac. A message will display in the installer window alerting you that your Mac will restart automatically. When your Mac restarts, it will be another several minutes before Mountain Lion is fully installed.

2 Optimize Your Data

M̲ost of us stockpile more data on our Macs than we know what to do with. We continually add to the heap when we download tempting new apps and music, as well as create data in Word documents, emails, and spreadsheets, and save photos. Leaving unwanted data on your computer will eat up Macintosh hard drive (HD) space and bog down your computer's resources. Lots of clutter also makes it difficult to find the files you want. Even if you have a huge amount of space on your Mac, if you can't quickly locate the stuff you need, you're probably not making the best use of your computer. This chapter will walk you through how to optimize your data by identifying some of the places obsolete data can hide, as well as show you how to make the most of the data you want to keep by creating a filing system that works for you.

> **Note** Throughout this chapter, we refer to the *Macintosh HD* to describe your hard drive—the place where most of your data is stored. You may have a Solid State Drive (SSD) on your Mac. Where we mention Macintosh HD, the same advice or instructions apply to a Mac with an SSD.

Delete Data You Don't Need

Some data accumulates without you knowing about it, as is the case with software updates and application support files that become outdated but hang around your Macintosh HD anyway. However, the most common type of data that takes up space on your computer is stuff you probably do know about, like your work documents, downloads from the Internet, and all of the thousands of image and music files you import into your favorite applications (see Figure 2-1). In this section we look at

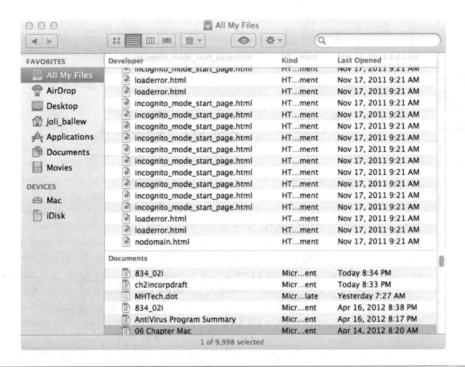

FIGURE 2-1 All My Files selected in List view, sorted by Application type

these more common types of data and consider which may be good candidates for removal. To get a glimpse of just how much data you have on your Macintosh HD, do the following:

1. Click Finder on the Dock.
2. Select All My Files in the sidebar.
3. Scroll through to get an idea of what you may want to delete.

Tip You can preview the contents of a file without opening it by using the Quick Look option in the Finder menu. It's the icon that looks like an eye. You can also preview your file by clicking it and pressing the SPACEBAR once.

Take advantage of the Arrange button in the Finder menu to display the contents in the window. When you click Arrange, you get a pop-up menu with options for displaying the files by kind, size, or date last opened. Sorting this way can help you identify files or folders you may want to cull. Very large files you either don't need

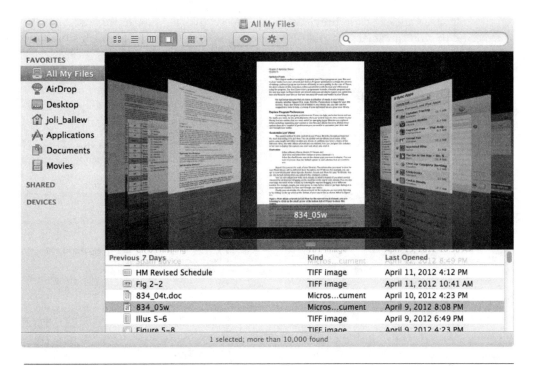

FIGURE 2-2   Documents display in Cover Flow view as small icons you can swipe through, like flipping through the pages of a book.

or haven't opened in a while are good candidates for removal. Remember to use the Arrange button to sort and display file contents when you go through each of the Finder areas in this chapter.

You can also view your files with gestures in Lion and Mountain Lion. When you select Cover Flow view in Finder, you can view your files as a row of icons that you gesture through with a horizontal two-finger swipe on your trackpad (or a horizontal one-finger swipe on your Magic Mouse), much as you do on an iPhone or iPad. Click the Cover Flow view button in your Finder, as shown in Figure 2-2, and use your trackpad or Magic Mouse to quickly flip through your files.

Documents

One of the most common places to find potentially unwanted data is in the Documents folder. Any files that you create, edit, and view, like Word or PDF documents, live in your Documents folder. Many applications use Documents as the default folder, so you may have more files in here than you realize. If you aren't sure about the contents of a file, use Quick Look to preview them. Once you locate files or folders you want to get rid of, you can select several files at once and drag them to the Trash simultaneously.

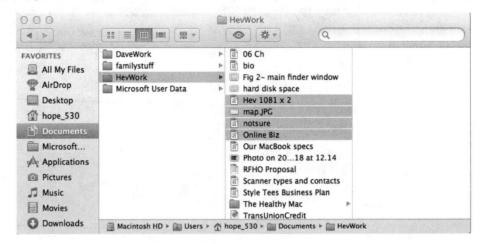

To select several documents to delete:

1. SHIFT-click to select the first and last items to create a selection of contiguous files, then release. You should see the selection highlighted.
2. If you want to select noncontiguous files, press the COMMAND key, click the files you want, and then release.
3. Drag the highlighted selection to the Trash.

Caution   Back up your Macintosh before you work through the suggestions on deleting data in this chapter. You might inadvertently delete data you want. If you aren't sure about how to perform a backup, review "Back Up to Time Machine" in Chapter 1 now.

Downloads

Files of all types show up in your Downloads folder when you click an email attachment (photo, PDF, Word document) or download an application installer like Oovoo. If you do nothing with these files, they remain in your Downloads folder and just take up space. Take a look at this area in your Finder for redundant files or for items you want to keep but file elsewhere. You may even be surprised that you have multiple copies of a single download because you absentmindedly clicked several times while waiting for a download.

Tip   Rather than opening your attachments straight from email, use Quick Look to preview the contents and then save them to an appropriate folder straight away.

Before you decide to delete items from the Downloads folder, check that you have them, if you want them, in one of your other folders. For example, if you downloaded a PDF manual for a project you are working on, check that you have a copy of the PDF in your project folder in Documents (or wherever else you keep your work) before you send the copy in the Downloads folder to the Trash.

Movies

The Movies folder may contain raw footage of videos you took with your camera, projects you created with iMovie, or source files like images and music you use to create your iMovie projects. These file types take up a huge amount of space on your hard drive and make them good candidates for removal or archiving; one ten-minute project can take 2 to 3GB of space! Once you complete an iMovie project, you may have clips that you didn't include in a project. If you don't think you'll use the footage, get rid of it by dragging it to the Trash. Make note of those you want to keep, either to use again or archive (which we explore at the end of the chapter).

Tip   Create a folder called Archive and drag files you want to keep but don't often use to this folder as you work through the steps in the following sections.

Music

You'll find a variety of media in your Music folder including your iTunes purchases (music, podcasts, audio books, and so on), as well as tracks from CDs that you ripped to your computer. The majority of these files are easier to manage in iTunes, which will be more thoroughly explored in Chapter 5. In the meantime, here are a few things to keep in mind.

For most users, the Music folder is the default location for your iTunes Media folder, which contains all the music, podcasts, apps, and other media that you download from the iTunes Store or copy from a disc. You want to check your default Media folder location, because any file you delete from the Music folder (if it's your default Media folder) will be permanently deleted from your iTunes library. However, even after you delete a file, it will still appear in your library but you'll be unable to play it—which makes things very confusing indeed.

To find where your iTunes Media folder is, do the following:

1. Launch iTunes and select Preferences from the iTunes menu.
2. Click the Advanced tab.
3. Make note of the iTunes Media folder location at the top of the dialog box, as shown in the illustration.

Advanced Preferences

General Playback Sharing Store Parental Devices Advanced

iTunes Media folder location

/Users/hope_530/Music/iTunes/iTunes Media   Change... / Reset

☑ Keep iTunes Media folder organized
Places files into album and artist folders, and names the files based on the disc number, track number, and the song title.

☑ Copy files to iTunes Media folder when adding to library

Reset all dialog warnings: Reset warnings
Reset iTunes Store cache: Reset cache

☐ Keep Mini Player on top of all other windows
☐ Keep movie window on top of all other windows

⑦   Cancel   OK

There are still some files that you may want to consider deleting in your Music folder, including old iTunes library files. More recent versions of iTunes create copies of the database that lists your media files in iTunes when you update the application.

After several updates, consider deleting these unnecessary files. Although each file is only a few megabytes, you can declutter your Music folder by removing them:

1. Click your Music folder.
2. Click Previous iTunes Libraries.
3. Select and drag old libraries to the Trash.

Pictures

Your Pictures folder stores all the photos and videos you download from your camera, iPhone, or email, as well as any projects you create with iPhoto. If you regularly download all your photos (even the bad ones) from your camera or iDevice, then you probably need to take a look at these files and decide if there are some you can delete. If your camera is able to take very high-resolution photographs, then deleting a few hundred unwanted images could save you several gigabytes of space and make organizing the photos you want that much easier.

Start your search for unwanted images in the Pictures folder itself. There may be a number of folders or perhaps just a long list of images that are not organized in any way. You can send a selection of photos to the Trash with the Action menu. With a selection highlighted, select Move to Trash from the Action menu, and all of the files will be sent to the Trash at the same time.

Next, launch iPhoto and browse through the images or projects you created there and identify those you can live without. While you're still in the program, select the ones you don't want and press DELETE.

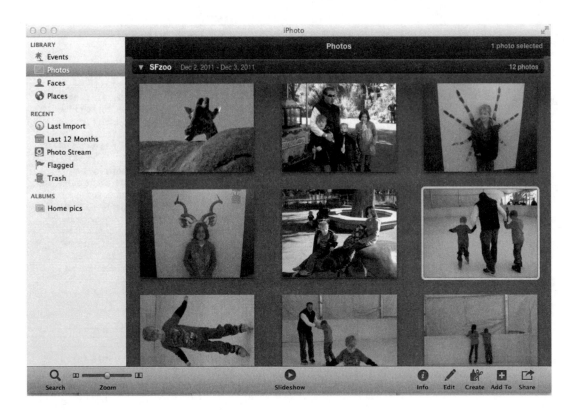

Note that the iPhoto library images must be deleted from within the iPhoto application. Images in the iPhoto application can't be permanently removed with the desktop Trash. To permanently delete the images you no longer want:

1. Select an image or images you want to remove.
2. Go to the iPhoto menu and select Empty iPhoto Trash.
3. Click OK when the dialog box appears.

Finally, if you have other image-editing software programs on your computer, check the files associated with that application and see if there are any that need cleaning up.

Public and Shared Folders

If you have more than one computer in your home or office (either another Mac or perhaps a PC) on your network, you probably made use of a Public folder to share your files with these other computers (see Figure 2-3). After the other user on the

FIGURE 2-3   Files in your Public folder that you share with other users on your network

network has accessed the files you want to share, consider deleting the files you copied to the network.

1. Click your Home folder.
2. Click the Public folder.
3. Select and delete redundant or obsolete files.

In addition, if you have more than one user account on an individual Mac, you have a Shared folder on your hard drive. Let's say you have a Kids user account and a Parent user account. The Parent user moves media from the Music folder to the Shared folder, and the Kids users can access the media in that folder (as can any other users who share the Mac); see Figure 2-4. If you decide that you don't want to grant access to the other user or that nobody wants the data in the shared folder any longer, delete the files by following these steps:

1. Click Finder.
2. Click Macintosh HD and then select the Shared folder.
3. Select the items you want to delete and drag them to the trash.

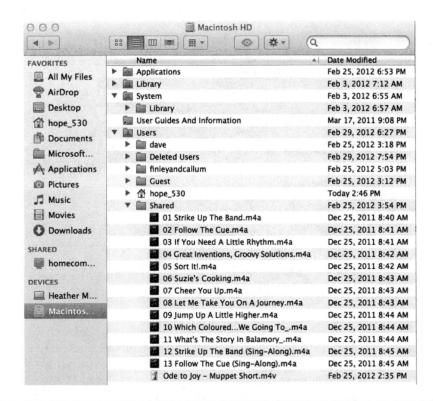

FIGURE 2-4   Files in the Shared folder on your hard drive that you share with other user accounts on your Mac

If you don't yet have a Public folder enabled or more than one user account on your Mac, you can jump to Chapter 9 to learn how to do this. If you wait to do this, which is fine, just keep in mind that these are places that can potentially accumulate lots of duplicate data.

Clean Up Aliases

Aliases enable you to access a particular file, folder, or application in several places at once. They aren't copies of the original item, and they actually take up very little space on your Mac but can clutter up your workspace. They are easy to spot in your folders or on your desktop as they have a little arrow in the lower-left corner. The icons in your Dock are another example of aliases; they are a link to the application, not the application itself. If you've created more aliases than you use or have aliases that are no longer working, you can work more efficiently without them.

Check that the aliases you have work, both in terms of taking you to the file or folder you want, but also that they make sense for how you work on your computer each day. For example, if you created aliases for a project you worked on but now you have completed that project, you can delete the alias on your desktop or in Finder.

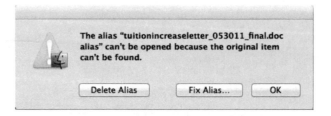

FIGURE 2-5   A broken alias will return this message when you click it. You can delete it or click Fix Alias to try to find the original file. If a file isn't found, you can opt to link the alias to a new file.

Aliases can break when the application or file they are linked to is deleted on a disc or drive that isn't on your computer, or be corrupted in some other way (see Figure 2-5).

Clean the Nooks and Crannies

In this section we look at data you may not be aware of, like temporary and preference files, as well as data from long-forgotten, and deleted, users. Many of these files reside on your Macintosh HD, and we'll look at some of the folders there more closely. However, it's important to note that there are many folders on your Macintosh HD that shouldn't be moved, deleted, or altered in any way. For example, with very few exceptions (none of which we'll look at here), it's a good idea to leave your System folder alone.

Temporary Files

Temporary files are created by some applications, such as MS Word, to back up your document while you are working in case of a crash. They can be generated from other programs as well, but all will have the .tmp extension. Temporary files should be deleted automatically when you quit the program, but for various reasons they aren't always deleted. These files can accumulate over a period of time and gunk up your Macintosh HD. Keep an eye out for file types with the extension .tmp while you work through some of the folders in this section.

> **Note**   One of the most plentiful types of temporary files is cache files, which are generated by Safari as you browse the Internet. These can accumulate quite quickly and need to be cleaned out periodically. How to do this will be explored in detail in Chapter 7.

Macintosh HD, Library, and Other Areas

Take a look at some of these less-visited areas on your Mac, like the Library, and you may be surprised at the number of obsolete and unnecessary files there. Your Library stores files that support applications you use. If you deleted an application, you can delete the files that supported that application. We'll take a look at Preference files shortly, but for now, check in the following folders for obsolete files that reside in the Library folder. (You can get to the Library by clicking Macintosh HD in the Finder and clicking Library.)

- Application Support
- Contextual Menu Items
- Input Methods

Preference Files

Preference files are stored in your Library folder and retain information about the customized settings you chose for an application (see Figure 2-6). After you delete an application, the preference files associated with that application remain on your Mac

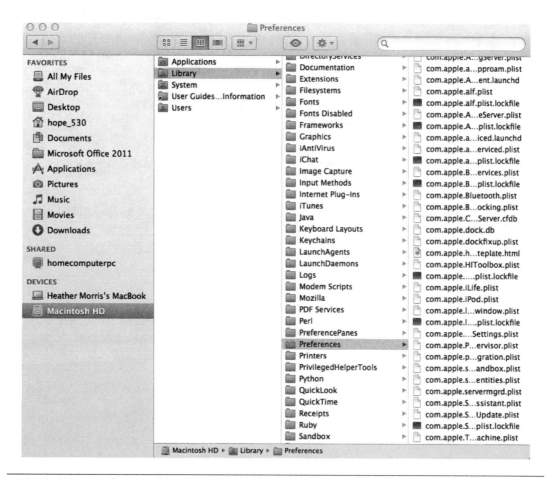

FIGURE 2-6   Preference files have the extension .plist.

Problematic Preference Files

Preference files can become corrupted and cause serious mischief with your programs. For example, a corrupt preference file can cause a program to crash when it opens, or when a document is saved, as well as a host of other annoying behaviors. If you find that a program is behaving erratically, you can troubleshoot the application by deleting a preference file. Log in to a different user account and open the program to see if the same problem occurs with the different user account. If it doesn't, the problem could be with the preference files for your specific user account. To see if this is indeed the problem, log back in to your account and drag the preference files for the problematic program to the Trash. Finally, restart the program and check to see if the problems you had are still occurring. If the same problems continue, recover the preference files from the Trash and continue troubleshooting.

and do very little for you. In general, they don't take up very much space, but you can delete these obsolete files to degunk your computer. To purge the files from your Mac, you need to delete them manually after you delete an application, if your application didn't come with an uninstaller. If the application came with an uninstaller, launching that will take care of both the application and all of its associated files—including preference files. To get rid of the files manually:

1. Open Finder and click the Macintosh HD icon.
2. Click the Library folder and the Preferences folder.
3. Scroll through the list and delete files that belong to programs you've deleted.

 Don't delete preference files if you don't know what application they belong to.

Deleted User Account Files

If you created temporary accounts on your Mac for visiting friends or relatives, you probably deleted them after they were no longer in use. However, a deleted user account may still contain data that takes up space on your Mac unless you get rid of it for good.

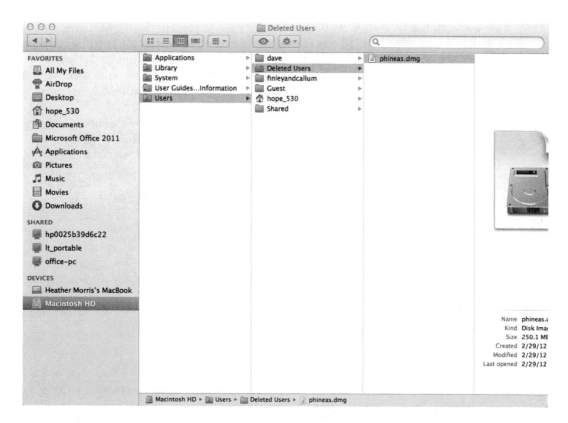

While older operating systems wouldn't allow the admin user to drag these files to the Trash, you can now do just that. If there is a chance you want to save the data, consider archiving the files and saving it to an external drive or DVD. To locate and delete data from a deleted user account:

1. Open the Finder.
2. Click Macintosh HD.
3. Click the Users folder.
4. Click the Deleted Users folder and select the file(s) that you want to delete.
5. CONTROL-click and then select Move to Trash.

Create an Organizational System

Mac OS X comes with a logical file system, which you can take advantage of to organize your own data. Each time you open a Finder window, you are presented with several navigation options in the sidebar under Favorites including Desktop, Home, Applications, Documents, Downloads, Movies, and possibly more depending on whether you added folders to the sidebar yourself. These items in your sidebar are shortcuts to each of these folders on your computer. Your Home folder is the one with a small house icon on it and your user name or the name you entered when you first set up your Mac. The best place to organize your own data is within the folders in your Home folder because your data will be easier to find, and many of the applications on your Mac use these folders as the default folder for saving or opening files. In Mountain Lion, you see the folders that are shown in Figure 2-7.

Note If you have lots of folders stored on your desktop, not only will it impede your ability to locate the files you want, but it will noticeably slow down Finder's performance. Folders on your Desktop are viewed by Finder as windows, and the more windows are open, the more slowly your Finder will respond.

Create Folders and Subfolders

To take advantage of the filing system on your OS X machine, you can create your own subfolders in a way that makes sense to you. For example, if you regularly create text documents for work, create a folder for those in Documents in your Home folder. You can then create your own filing system by year, event, project, or anything else that will help you find your files easily. To create a new folder, click the Action menu (the one that looks like a gear) and select New Folder.

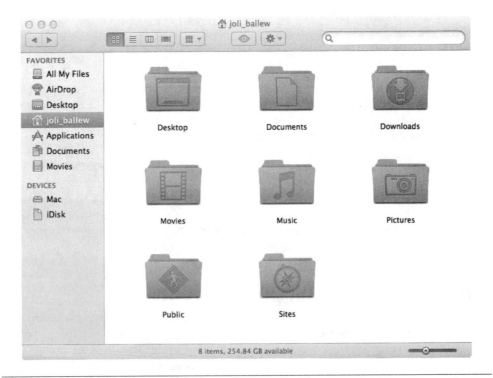

FIGURE 2-7 The Home folder in Mountain Lion with all the folders you need to organize your data

If you find a number of files you want to move to a new folder, you can create a selection and create a new folder at the same time. With this shortcut, the files hop into their new home before your eyes. To create a new folder with a selection of files:

1. Select the files you want to move.
2. CONTROL-click to get the contextual menu.
3. Select New Folder with Selection.

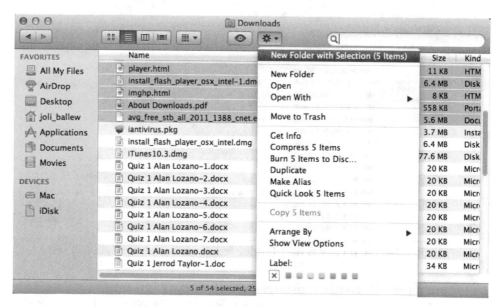

4. Name your folder.

Place Data in the Proper Folders

While you were reviewing the many folders and your Mac's Home folder in the earlier activities in this chapter, you may have noticed image files showing up in your Documents folder or some other item residing where it should not. There may be some reason you saved a movie to your Documents folder but, if there isn't, consider moving the file to its proper home in the Movies folder.

Create Smart Folders with Spotlight

If you can't break yourself of the habit of navigating to your files through Spotlight, you can put Spotlight to work as a sort of filing assistant by working with and creating Smart Folders. A *Smart Folder* is a type of folder that updates its contents based on search criteria you set. For example, if you search Spotlight for files that you've created in the last month, you can create a Smart Folder based on that, as well as adding additional

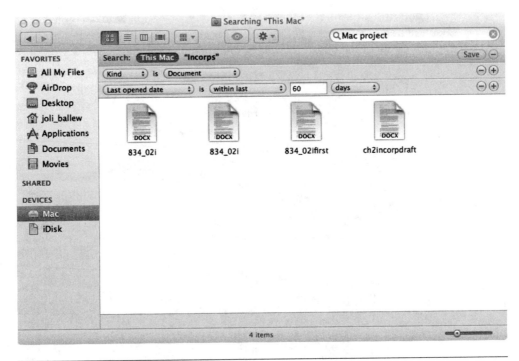

FIGURE 2-8 Create a Smart Folder based on search criteria you set.

criteria like file type or name (see Figure 2-8). Once you create a Smart Folder, you can include it in the sidebar of your Finder. To create a Smart Folder:

1. Open a Finder window and enter a search term in the Spotlight window.
2. Click the plus (+) symbol beneath the search window to add criteria. You can select from Kind, Last Opened Date, Last Modified Date, Created Date, Name, and Contents.
3. Select an option from the pop-up menu next to the criteria you selected. For instance, if you selected Kind, you can choose Document, Image, PDF, Music, and more.
4. Click the plus (+) symbol to add another search criteria if you want. You can select from Last Opened Date, Last Modified Date, or Created Date.
5. Select an option from the adjoining pop-up menu to set the date range; for example, within the last five days, two weeks, three months, and so on.
6. When you are finished defining the search criteria for your Smart Folder, click Save under the Spotlight window. Name your folder by typing over the characters in the Save As box and click Save. The file will be automatically added to your sidebar by default.

Note You can also create a Smart Folder in the Finder by clicking File and selecting New Smart Folder.

To edit your Smart Folder, select it in the sidebar and click the Action menu. From this menu, click Show Search Criteria. You can also CONTROL-click or right-click and select Show Search Criteria. Once you have the search criteria for the folder in front of you, add or delete any of the criteria you want to change. Click Save when you finish.

If you want to delete the Smart Folder, press COMMAND and drag the folder out of the sidebar.

When to Move and When to Copy

Think carefully about whether you really want to copy your files and folders or simply move them to a more logical location in your Home folder. If the file in question is one that you need to work on and update regularly, it will be difficult to manage the changes in two separate locations. Two files also take up more space on your hard drive. If you need to access the data from more than one location, it's easier and more efficient to create an alias of the file. There are several ways to move and copy your files on your Mac.

To move a file, folder, or a selection:

- Click and drag it into another Finder window on your computer. Note that if the original folder and destination folder are on different drives, the file will automatically be copied.
- Click the file and press COMMAND-C. Open a window you want to move the file into and press COMMAND-OPTION-V (this will move the file to the new location).

To copy a file:

- Press CONTROL-click and select Copy from the contextual menu. Press COMMAND-V to copy the file into a new Finder window. The filename will be appended with "copy." You can rename the file if you want.
- Press COMMAND-C, then COMMAND-V, to copy the file to a new window.

 The OPTION-COMMAND-V shortcut to move your file will only work if you have Lion or Mountain Lion OS X. If you are running an older system, you won't be able to use this shortcut.

Create New Aliases

One benefit of aliases is they won't take much space on your Mac—certainly not as much as copying the originals in multiple locations, which isn't always a great idea for reasons beyond space. Aliases act as a link between the original file, folder, or application and the location where you want those items to open. If you are not quite sure if you want to move an item from its present location, it may be simplest just to make an alias of the folder in another window.

If you have a file or application that you want quick access to, you can create an alias of that item and place it in another location on your Mac. Maybe you're building a basic web page with iWeb, and want access to the iPhoto application so you can edit the photos you want for your site. You can create an alias of iPhoto and place it in your iWeb folder or in some other folder where you keep your other files for your website project.

To create an alias of a file or folder:

1. Select the item in the window by clicking it.
2. Select Make Alias from the Action menu. Your Mac will keep the filename the same but add "alias" to the end of it. You can type over the name if you prefer not to have the word "alias" in the filename.
3. Drag the alias to a location of your choice.
4. Rename the alias if you want.

Tip You can press COMMAND-OPTION and drag the file out of the window and into another window to make an alias without having to rename it.

Compress and Archive Rarely Used Data

As you worked through this chapter, you probably noticed a number of files and folders that you didn't want to delete but that you don't really use or need very often. If you want to hold on to that data but also save a little space and get organized, you can compress the data and archive it on your Mac, on an external drive, or on a DVD or CD. You can create a main archive folder and data and move your data into that or create a compressed file. To compress a file:

1. Select a file or files to compress.
2. Select Compress from the Action menu or CONTROL-click the file or files.

3. Move the archived file to your external drive or a disc.

To expand the file back to the original size, double-click the .zip file.

 If you compress one file, the compressed file has the name of its original file but with a .zip extension. If you select and compress several files at once, the file is called Archive.zip.

Empty the Trash

All your hard work deleting and organizing your Mac has probably resulted in a very full Trash folder. To clear room on your Mac for new data, be sure to empty the Trash. You can do this by selecting Empty Trash from the Finder or by double-clicking the Trash icon and clicking Empty. However, you should keep in mind that once you empty the Trash the file or files aren't completely gone from your Mac. The space occupied by the deleted files becomes available to be overwritten—which takes time to do. Until the files are overwritten, someone could restore the data in them with recovery software.

If you delete potentially sensitive personal information and want to ensure that nobody can recover it, choose Secure Empty Trash from the Finder. This option will completely overwrite your deleted data and make it impossible for anyone to read.

 The Trash folder is not the only place on your Mac where unwanted data lives. As you saw with iPhoto, some applications have their own Trash folders. Mail is another example of this and will be explored in Chapter 6.

3 Remove Unwanted Programs

With the ease of downloading programs from the App Store, from sources like CNET or from discs, it's not hard to find yourself with more applications than you can ever use. As with other unwanted items on your Mac, get rid of what you don't use to keep your Mac free of clutter, or simply to make room for downloading the latest version of Angry Birds or other similarly important applications.

Uninstall Unwanted Applications

In this section we take a look at how to remove applications you aren't using and want to get rid of. Some applications come with an uninstaller, and you should use this whenever you can. For applications without an uninstaller, you need to look for and delete the support files manually, which we explore in this first section.

 Caution As with any deletions you do on your Mac, always back up your Macintosh HD before making the changes suggested in this chapter.

Review the Applications Folder

Start your search for unwanted programs in your Applications folder in the Finder. Scroll through the list of applications and take note of any that you no longer use or want. Try viewing the files by Date Last Opened for an idea of when you may have last used the program (if at all).

Next, check to see if the application has a folder with the same name. Open the folder and look for an uninstaller. They usually have the application name on them and the word "uninstall" in the filename. If the application comes with its own uninstaller, you should use that to remove the application from your Mac.

You can also use Launchpad to remove applications that you bought through the App Store. Removing apps from Launchpad will be discussed shortly.

Uninstall Applications You Don't Want

If the application came with an uninstaller, click the uninstaller to launch it and follow the instructions. Uninstalling can usually be accomplished with just a few clicks, and the program, as well as the associated support files, will be removed from your Mac.

If the application does not come with an uninstaller, you can drag the application itself to the Trash. However, you want to look around for any files that belong to the application as well. Some applications themselves do not take up much space, but their support files can be very large indeed. GarageBand is an excellent example of this (see the following sidebar). To find related application files that you can delete, look in the Application Support folder (see Figure 3-1):

1. Click the Macintosh HD folder in the Finder.
2. Click Library and then Application Support.
3. Look for folders or files in the folder and drag them to the Trash.
4. Empty the Trash.

Note Applications that are distributed on CD or DVD or as disk images include an uninstaller. Put the disc in your Mac and click the Customize button to uninstall, or select Uninstall from the disc menu.

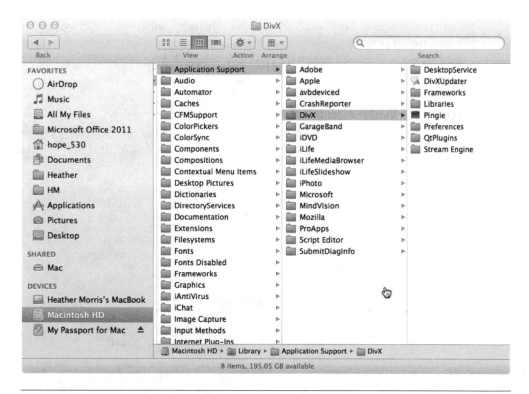

FIGURE 3-1   Navigate to the Application Support folder to identify files belonging to an application, which you can delete once you delete the application.

GarageBand

GarageBand is an application that comes with the iLife suite included on all brand-new Macs. iLife includes iPhoto and iMovie as well. GarageBand is a great program for learning how to play an instrument, or for composing and recording music. However, if your creative talents don't tend toward the musical, consider removing this application from your computer to save some space. GarageBand comes with a number of sample recordings of various instruments, called *loops*. These loops, found in the Application Support folder of your Library, are the largest part of the application. If you delete them, you'll be rewarded with an extra 1.5GB of space on your hard drive!

Uninstall Unwanted Hardware and Its Software

These days most hardware connects to our Macs wirelessly (printers, external hard drives, and even scanners), but you might still be using hardware that needs to connect physically to your Mac. When you buy new hardware, you often install software to allow the hardware to work correctly on your computer. Think about hardware that you currently use, but also remember whether you have removed any hardware on your Mac at some point in the past; for example, a scanner. Although the hardware may be gone, you may still have associated software on your hard disk that you need to remove.

Review Your Hardware

Look in the System Preferences pane under Hardware to see the devices currently connected to your Mac. You will see a list of printers and scanners on the left side of the window.

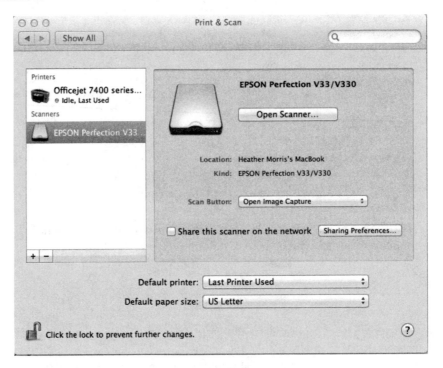

If you find a printer or scanner that you don't use or want to remove, follow these steps:

1. Click the System Preferences icon.
2. Click Print & Scan.
3. Click the hardware and click the minus (–) sign.
4. Click Delete Printer or Delete Scanner when prompted.

Note   For a flash drive, you can simply drag its icon to the Trash. When you do, the Trash icon will change to an arrow and you can safely remove the drive.

Remove Applications Related to Hardware You No Longer Own

When you connect hardware, you often install related software on your Mac (usually via an optical disc) that enables the device to work on your computer. A common type of software is called *drivers*, which enable your Mac to identify and communicate with a hardware device. Your Mac needs a suitable driver to be able to use each device. Once you safely remove your hardware, look for and delete the software that came with your device.

As with other application types, you may have an uninstaller that removes the application and files, or you may need to manually delete the application and files that relate to the hardware. First check if the supporting software has its own uninstaller, and then do the following to remove the device software as shown in Figure 3-2:

1. Go to Macintosh HD and select Library.
2. Click the Printers folder to look for a device that is no longer connected to your Mac, such as a printer or scanner.
3. Drag the folder to the Trash.

Note there are also files in the Printers folder in the Library, called PPDs (PostScript Printer Definitions), which relate to printers you connect to your Mac. The folder contains PostScript Printer Definition files that tell OS X which features particular printers have. For example, you have files for a number of printer models from Canon, Epson, HP, and more. While you may not have these printers connected to your Mac at present, the files are worth keeping in case you do connect a different printer to your computer in the future—even temporarily. They are also small files and you won't save much space by deleting them.

FIGURE 3-2   Support file for a scanner no longer connected to the computer

Explore Launchpad and Mission Control

Two new features that arrived on your desktop in Lion are Launchpad and Mission Control. Launchpad is a new way of accessing your applications and all of their folders and will seem very familiar to those with an iPhone, iPod touch, or iPad as the screen is almost identical to a Home screen on one of these iDevices. Mission Control is a way to view your current desktop, all the applications, and any associated windows you have open. Launchpad and Mission Control are both useful tools to manage your applications and desktop while you work. The icons for these features are shown here, and you'll see them in your Dock.

In Launchpad, you can view all the applications that you downloaded through the App Store, applications that came with your Mac, as well as those from other sources—all arranged in a neat array of icons. Launchpad looks like the Home screen on an iOS device. You can access the Launchpad by clicking the little spaceship icon in your Dock or through a number of other shortcuts or gestures. For example, the default gesture for accessing Launchpad is a four-finger "pinch." Place four fingers on a trackpad and pinch them together. You should see the screen shown in Figure 3-3.

FIGURE 3-3 The Launchpad screen with all your app icons arranged neatly in rows like the Home screen on an iOS device.

The icons on Launchpad are arranged by Apple apps first and then by any third-party applications you downloaded. You may have more than one Launchpad screen depending on the number of apps you have. If you have more than one screen, you'll see small white dots (two, three, or even more) beneath the icons. The brightest dot is the active screen, the one you are currently on. To switch between Launchpad screens, use a two-finger sideways swipe on your trackpad or click one of the white dots to move to the next screen.

Mission Control is a handy tool that allows you to view everything your Mac is doing right now. Apple describes Mission Control as "Mac command central." You get a quick view of all the windows open on your desktop, displayed in stacks by application type, as well as a view of your Dashboard. If you click an application icon, Mission Control will bring the application and all of its open windows to the foreground. You can start Mission Control in a number of ways:

- Click the Mission Control Dock icon.
- Make a three-finger upward swipe on a trackpad
- Use a hot corner you configure in Preferences
- Press CONTROL and the up arrow key
- Use a shortcut that you configure

Mission Control is arranged by the following features, as shown in Figure 3-4:

- Spaces run along the top of the window. You can have up to 16 Spaces on your Mac, which act like virtual desktops, all running at the same time. If you have an application open in full-screen mode, one of the Spaces will be automatically assigned to the application. You can add a Space by pointing your cursor in the upper-right corner of Mission Control and clicking the plus + symbol. You can assign a different application to each Space and navigate between the Spaces by swiping three fingers across your trackpad, or launching Mission Control and clicking the desktop you want.
- The Dashboard is the default space in the top left of the Mission Control screen. Your Dashboard is home to all your widgets—all the small applications that you use to do things like look up an address, check the weather, or play a game.
- Application windows show both the applications currently running as well as the windows open in that application. You can point your cursor to one of the windows within Mission Control to open it or preview it by hovering the cursor over it and pressing the SPACEBAR. The active window will be the one highlighted by a blue border.

Note   Customizing your Mission Control screen and configuring Spaces and your Dashboard will be explored more thoroughly in Chapter 4.

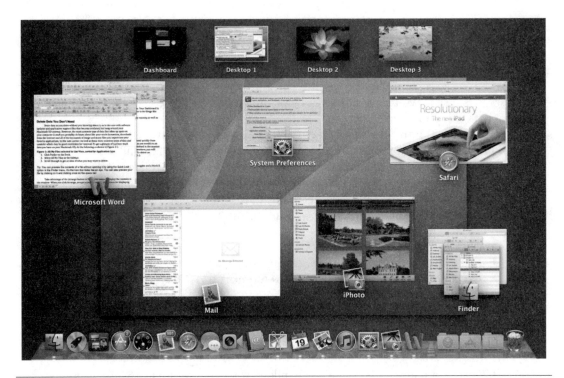

FIGURE 3-4   The Mission Control screen with Spaces running along the top, including the Dashboard as well as all of your open applications and all of their open windows

Use Launchpad to Remove Apps You Don't Use

Any app that you bought through Apple's App Store can be deleted quickly from your Mac on the Launchpad screen. You interact with the icons much as you would on an iOS device. Note that only apps bought through the App Store can be deleted in the manner outlined next. If you have third-party applications you purchased elsewhere, you will have to remove them as you do other applications on your computer. To delete an application from Launchpad:

1. Start Launchpad and drag the application icon to the Trash.
   Or:
2. Click and hold on an application icon and wait until the icon wiggles and a black X appears.
3. Click the X in the left corner of the application icon.
4. Click Delete when prompted to permanently delete the application.

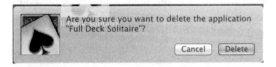

If you decide later that you still want the application, you can reinstall it from the App Store. Once you buy an app, you can reinstall it again without paying.

Check for Malware and Remove It

Speaking of applications you don't want, malware has become more of a problem for Mac users in recent years, and that trend is likely to continue. Malware is a malicious application that comes in many forms and can cause problems on your Mac, ranging from slightly annoying to downright dangerous to your computer and the security of your personal information. Here is a breakdown of the most common types of malware:

- Adware falls into the annoying category of malware. Once your Mac is infected with adware, you will be plagued with pop-up or pop-under windows advertising things you have no interest in.
- Spyware can pose a more serious threat to your personal information. Spyware can collect information about you without you knowing about it, like which web sites you visit, your login names and passwords, and even your bank details.
- Trojan horses embed malicious software in another application that you download onto your computer. You are tricked into downloading something that looks legitimate but carries malware in it intended to mine your computer for personal details or to take control of your computer for some other purpose.
- Viruses can harm your computer in a number of ways, including making changes to your data or deleting or damaging files on your computer. Once viruses are on your computer, they copy themselves and attach to other applications. Viruses spread from computer to computer (including Macs) via other applications that are infected.

Virus or Malware?

When talking about malware, people often use the terms "virus" and "malware" interchangeably. A virus is a type of malware that infects a computer when the user receives an infected file or application through email or through a server. Once the user opens the infected file, the virus runs and duplicates itself onto other files or applications on your Mac. If the virus attaches itself to a file on your computer, and you then send that file as an attachment to another computers user, you can spread the virus to them.

Malware (including spyware, adware, and Trojan horses) arrives on your Mac when *you* download it, usually when you download what you think is a safe application type on the Internet. Malware is usually hidden within other programs and operates without you knowing about it. Unfortunately, new types of malware are created all the time.

In addition to searching for and deleting malware on your Mac, there are a number of other steps you can take to protect your Mac and your personal data, including monitoring your email for suspicious mail attachments and changing your passwords on a regular schedule. These strategies and more will be outlined in Chapters 6, 7, and 13.

The best way to protect your Mac from malware is to monitor for it and remove it when you find it. There are a number of anti-malware programs that you can use on your Mac, many of them free. Note that while some are referred to as anti-virus software, most check for a range of malware. Apple does not have a general anti-malware application, though they did come up with one that dealt specifically with a widespread Trojan horse infection in the spring of 2011.

In general, you want an anti-malware program that scans for a wide range of malware and regularly updates malware definitions so the program can scan for the new types of malware that emerge frequently. Some programs update the definitions automatically and some require you to do this manually when you run a scan. Anti-malware programs can also consume a lot of your Mac's resources and slow you down while you are trying to work. Look for applications that can scan without taking up too much of your Mac's resources.

The four anti-malware programs listed here are ones that the authors have used, but there are others that are worth exploring as well.

- **iAntiVirus Free Edition** is free to download from www.iantivirus.com and scans for viruses, Trojans, spyware, and adware that are specific to the Mac. The program can isolate potential malware, which you can then delete. It can run in the background while you work and doesn't take up much of your Mac's resources. A normal scan can take up to an hour to complete, depending on how much data you have on your computer, and you can also choose to do a quick scan or a custom scan of some area of your computer. The company site says the program updates malware automatically, but it's unclear how often new definitions are added to their database. It has a simple interface, as shown here, and is easy to run.

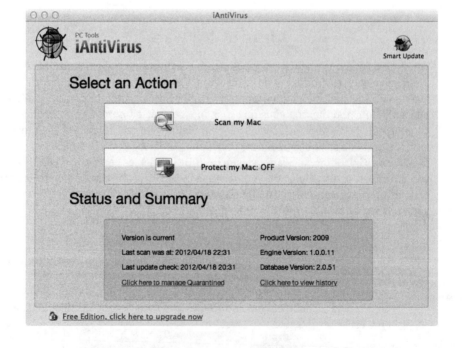

- **Sophos Anti-Virus for Mac Home Edition** is free to download from www
  .sophos.com or from cnet.com. The program updates virus definitions automatically
  and can scan while you work. It detects a range of both Mac and Windows malware,
  which is especially good if you have both types of computer on your network. It
  does slow your Mac down a little more than some of the other programs and can
  take a while to complete a scan but is not otherwise too intrusive.

- **VirusBarrier Plus** is a paid application ($9.99) that you can download through
  the App Store. According to the company site, it updates malware definitions
  twice a week and you can update those manually when you launch the
  application. You can perform scheduled scans or you can choose to scan folders
  and files manually. It slows down your Mac slightly while you work but doesn't
  interrupt most computing tasks. It is very simple to use and has an on-demand
  scanning option that allows you to drag a file or folder into the "on-demand"
  scanner, as shown in Figure 3-5.

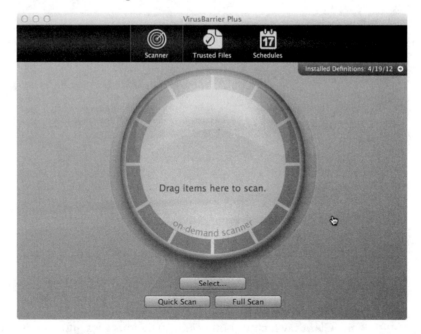

FIGURE 3-5   On-demand scanner in VirusBarrier Plus. Drag a selected file into
the program to scan or perform a full scan of your Mac.

- **ClamXav** is free to download through the App Store. It is an open source anti-malware program that scans for viruses and Trojans. You can update virus definitions manually after you launch the program and it will run scans of the files or folders you chose. The scans can run while you work without slowing down your computer too much, though a full scan can take a half an hour or more. It will quarantine suspicious items and you can delete them.

Once you download an anti-malware program, you can perform a scan and get rid of any malware the program finds. The example in Figure 3-6 is done with ClamXav (free to download in the App Store) and shows a type of email spam called *phishing*. These types of email try to get you to disclose some of your personal information, like an account number or password, by posing as a legitimate business. They don't generally contain malware, but you can delete them in ClamXav or via the Mail application.

To do a search for malware and remove it:

1. Start Launchpad and click ClamXav to start the program.
2. Click Update Definitions in the menu and wait while the application updates the malware definitions.
3. Select an area from the Source List in the left of the window. If you don't see a folder in the Source List you want to scan, click the plus (+) button at the bottom of the Source List to add a folder.

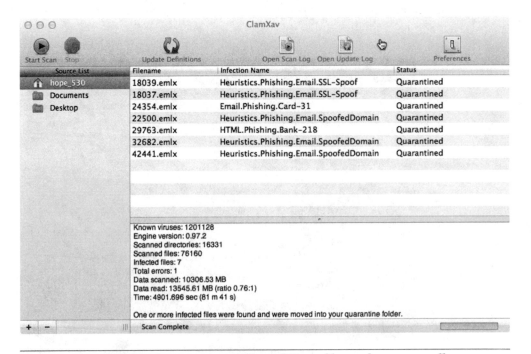

FIGURE 3-6   ClamXav locates potentially malicious files and you manually delete them.

4. Click Start Scan and wait while the application scans the files. The amount of time it takes to scan depends on the size of the folder you selected. You can work as you do normally while the program performs the scan.

5. When the program is done scanning, any infected files will appear in a list in the main window.

6. Select the file, click the File menu, select Infection List, and then select Show Path from the submenu. This will show you where the file is located on your computer.

7. To delete the file from within ClamXav, select the file by clicking it once. Next, click File in the menu, select Infection List, and then select Delete File from the submenu.

8. Empty the Trash on your desktop.

Once you learn how to use your anti-malware program, make sure you schedule regular scans and update the software frequently. The updates often contain information about new malware types and will scan for them once you update. In ClamXav, do the following to schedule malware definition updates and schedule regular scans of your Mac:

1. Open ClamXav and click the Preferences icon first (not shown), and then click the Schedule icon (shown).

2. Click the drop-down menu under Update Virus Definitions and select from one of the options, including: Weekdays, Weekends, or one day of the week.

3. Select a time of day for the program to update malware definitions by clicking on the up or down arrows.

4. Choose a day for the program to perform a scan of your computer. You can select a day of the week or Every Day, Weekends, and so on.
5. Select a time to schedule a scan by clicking the arrows.
6. Click OK when you are done.

Set Gatekeeper to Let Your Mac Download the Apps You Need

The most common route of infection for malware is via software you download onto your Mac. Apple attempted to deal with that when adding Gatekeeper to Mountain Lion, which effectively encourages users to download programs only through the App Store or through software developers who are part of Apple's developer program. The default setting on Gatekeeper prevents you from downloading software from other sources. If you want to change the settings so that you can download applications from anywhere on the Internet, you have to do so manually. To change Gatekeeper's settings:

1. Open System Preferences.
2. Click Security & Privacy and check you are in the General section by clicking that tab at the top (see Figure 3-7).

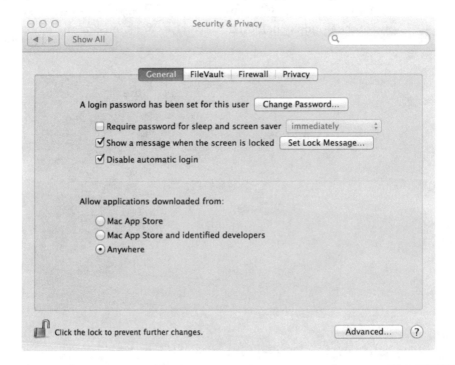

FIGURE 3-7   The download application options in Gatekeeper

3. Click the lock to unlock the screen and enter your admin password when prompted.
4. Select Allow Applications Downloaded from Anywhere. You will get a warning after selecting this option. To proceed, click the Allow From Anywhere button. If you want to keep the security settings suggested by Apple, click Cancel to revert to the default security settings.
5. Click the lock to secure these preferences, and then close the window.

Caution   If you select Anywhere as an option, you are taking a risk that your computer could be infected with malware. Applications from the App Store and identified developers should meet the needs of most users.

4 Make OS X Look and Work the Way You Prefer

The *graphical user interface (GUI)* that comes with OS X can be customized to look and work the way you want. GUI (pronounced gooey) refers to the visual features like icons, menus, lists, and so forth, that you interact with to start an application, find and use files, or play media on iTunes. The GUI makes it easy for you to do the things you want to do on your Mac, and no company has developed a more appealing or easier-to-use interface than Apple. This chapter will explore some of the ways you can tweak and customize these features in OS X to suit the way you work and to keep you organized.

 Mountain Lion is used throughout for the examples, but you'll be able to make many of the same changes with Lion. If you have an older OS X, you will have different features to work with and won't have things like Launchpad and Mission Control.

Optimize the Desktop

Whether you want to customize the images on your desktop or screensaver, or tidy up your work environment, this section will show you how to make the desktop your own. You'll also learn about how to configure hot corners to activate functions on your desktop, as well as customizing Notifications so that it functions the way you want and doesn't get in your way.

Make the Desktop Look the Way You Want

You can make your desktop look just about any way you want. Often a solid, neutral background is easier to negotiate and less noisy than some of the default Apple images that come with your Mac. Perhaps you want to really individualize your desktop and use a favorite vacation snap or photo of your family. To select a custom desktop image:

1. Click the System Preferences icon in the Dock or click the Apple menu and select System Preferences.
2. Click Desktop & Screen Saver.

3. Click through the folders on the left of the pane to find a source for your desktop image (see Figure 4-1).
4. Select one image by clicking it, or select an entire folder and select the check box next to Change picture to have the desktop picture change periodically. Once you select this option, click the pop-up menu to choose to have the picture rotated once a day, once an hour, or more frequently. You can also opt to have the desktop image change when you log in to your Mac or when your computer goes to sleep.

Note If you opt to use images that are not from the Apple folder but from iPhoto or other folders, a different pop-up menu will display. Images in these locations often won't have the exact dimensions that fit your screen (as the preformatted Apple desktop images do), so you need to tell OS X how to display them. For example, you can opt to have the image fill the screen, center on the screen, or stretch to fill the screen.

FIGURE 4-1 Choose a desktop image from the Apple folder, your iPhoto folder, or another folder on your Mac.

After you select a desktop image, consider whether you want a translucent or solid menu bar for the desktop. If you opt for a translucent menu, you can see through the menu bar and still make out the details of your desktop image. On the other hand, translucent menu bars sometimes make it difficult for the farsighted among us to make out all those tiny little menu icons (or menulets or as they are sometimes called). Choose what works for you and either select or deselect the Translucent menu bar check box in the Desktop Preferences pane.

Configure Hot Corners

When you configure a hot corner, you set your Mac to activate a certain function when you park your cursor in one of the four corners of your desktop. For example, if you want to step away from your Mac, you can either put your Mac to sleep or activate a screensaver to keep your work hidden from nosy neighbors or family members. You can set hot corners for your computer in two ways: through the Desktop & Screen Saver Preferences panes or through the Mission Control Preferences pane. Other options for hot corners include

- **Mission Control** If you don't have a trackpad, it may be handy to have another way to launch Mission Control.
- **Application Windows** This hot corner is like Exposê (which is missing in Mountain Lion). With this hot corner configured, you can view all the windows that are open in one application. When you park your cursor in the corner you configure, you see all the windows for a given application. You can cycle through your open applications by pressing the TAB key.
- **Desktop** Clear all of the open windows off your desktop to see what's there.
- **Put Display to Sleep** Sleep mode gives your Mac a periodic rest and uses a lot less energy than running a flashy screen saver. You can also configure security settings requiring a password to wake your screen up.

To set the hot corners:

1. Click System Preferences and select Desktop & Screen Saver.
2. Select Screen Saver and click Hot Corners.
3. Click one of the pop-up menus to select an option for that corner, as shown in the illustration.
4. Repeat the process for other corners if you want and then click OK.

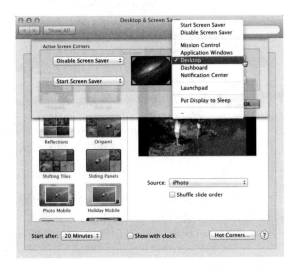

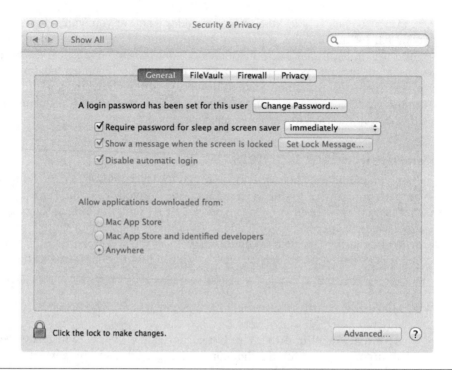

FIGURE 4-2 Require a password to wake up your display or to deactivate the screen saver.

If you choose to configure a hot corner to put your display to sleep, which is a good option if you want to consume less energy, you can require a password to activate the display to keep your data safe while you are away from your Mac. To enable the password option:

1. Click the System Preferences in the Dock or click the Apple menu and select Preferences.
2. Click Security & Privacy and check that the General tab is selected (see Figure 4-2).
3. Select the check box next to Require password for sleep and screen saver.
4. Select a time option from the pop-up menu. You can choose to require a password as soon as your display sleeps or within a few minutes or an hour or more.
5. Close the Preferences window when you are done.

Configure Notification Center

If you have an iPhone, some of the features of Notification Center will feel familiar to you. This new feature in Mountain Lion notifies you when you have new mail, messages, missed FaceTime calls, upcoming events in iCal, and more. The notifications catch your attention with small alert boxes that pop up on your screen to let you know of activity in some or all of your applications—you decide which ones you want to include in Notifications and how the boxes behave. There is a new icon in your menu bar next to Spotlight that looks like a small bulleted list, which you can click to view your notifications. To configure Notifications for your desktop:

1. Click the System Preferences in the Dock or click the Apple menu and select Preferences.
2. Click Notifications in the Preferences pane.
3. Click an application in the left side of the window.
4. Select an alert style for the application. You can choose None to have no notification for the app, or choose Banners (which means that the alert appears on your screen for a few seconds and then disappears), or choose Alerts, which means that the alert remains on your screen until you close it.
5. Select the number of notifications you want for the application by clicking the pop-up menu next to the check box Show in Notification Center (1, 5, 10, or 20 Recent Items).

6. Repeat this process for each of the applications.

Personalize the Dock

The Dock is an efficient, one-click way to access all the applications, utilities, documents, and folders that you use most frequently. The icons are shortcuts to your favorite applications or folders. The Dock gathers your applications to the left of a vertical dashed line, while Stacks, files, folders, minimized windows, and the Trash reside on the right.

When an application is open, a small blue dot appears beneath the application icon in the dock. If you open an application that isn't in the Dock, its icon will appear there while it is open. You can customize what you want to appear in the Dock, where you want it to appear, and even where you want the Dock to appear on your desktop.

Add and Remove Dock Icons

Customize your Dock by populating it with the features you use the most. It is a straightforward process of dragging and dropping an icon from a window or folder, and releasing it into the Dock. You can also start Launchpad and select an item from the Launchpad screen to drag into the Dock. Choose where you want it to go by placing it between two existing Dock icons.

Need to remove an icon? Click and drag it up and out of the Dock and it vanishes in a puff of smoke (literally, try it!). Don't worry, though, as the item you vaporized can still be found in its home folder.

You can also organize the icons within the Dock in a way that makes the most sense to you. Click and drag an icon horizontally across the Dock and release it where you want it to be.

Note You can drag applications from your application folder into the Dock if you don't see them in Launchpad.

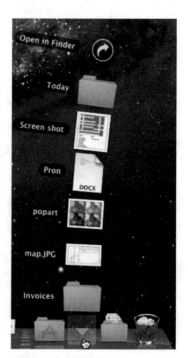

Create Your Own Dock Stacks

Stacks are what pop up when you click a folder in the Dock. You have two ready-made Stacks (Downloads and Documents) in your Dock, but you can create your own as well. Stacks make it easy to open frequently used files within your favorite folders. You may see a fan of files curving up to the right, as shown in the illustration, or you can customize your stacks to display in Grid view or List view if you prefer. To open and use one of the files in the Stack, click it once and you're in business.

To create your own Stack, open your Finder and locate a folder that you work with frequently and want to have in a stack on your Dock. Click and drag the icon to the right side of the Dock next to the other folders to create a new Stack. To change how you view your Stack:

1. Right-click or CONTROL-click the folder in the Dock.
2. Select Fan, Grid, or List from the pop-up list.

Note To remove a stack from the Dock, drag it to the Trash.

Enlarge, Reposition (Magnify), or Hide the Dock

You can alter the Dock in a number of ways including increasing the size of the Dock icons, moving it to a different part of your desktop, or hiding it and using it only when you need it. You can also tweak the icons to display in a magnified state when you point your cursor at them. Most of these adjustments can be made in your System Preferences pane. Go to System Preferences, select Dock, and do the following:

1. Move the Size slider bar to the right to increase the Dock size.
2. Select a different position (Left, Right) to display the Dock if you want.

Experiment with the sliders and watch for the effects on your Dock as you make adjustments—you'll see the results instantly. If you find the Dock gets in your way while you work, you can select "Automatically hide and show the Dock" to hide it while you're working. If you opt for this approach, the dock will pop up only when you move your cursor to the bottom of the screen.

Tip In Lion and Mountain Lion, you can adjust the size of your Dock by hovering the cursor over the thin vertical line in the Dock. When a double arrow appears, click and move your mouse up to enlarge the Dock or down to reduce it.

If you want to see magnified Dock icons when you point your cursor over them, select Magnification and adjust the slider to the right to increase the size of the icons. Setting this slider to "Max" will provide you with very large icons when you hover your cursor over them, as shown in Figures 4-3 and 4-4.

Finally, you can adjust the icons in the Dock from contextual menus. CONTROL-click or right-click to display the contextual menu for the Dock items. You can select Show

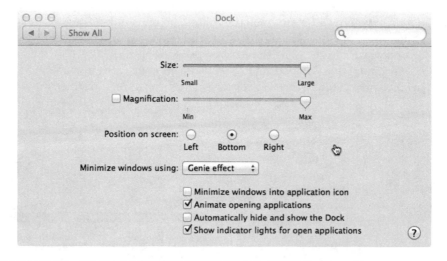

FIGURE 4-3 Change the size and position of the Dock on your screen.

FIGURE 4-4   If you select Magnification, your Dock icons will become magnified when you point your cursor at them, as shown here.

All Windows, Hide, and Quit from a pop-up menu or select from the Options submenu: Remove from Dock, Open at Login, or Show in Finder.

Make the Finder More Efficient to Use

The Finder is central to your Mac's GUI, and it's where you locate most of your stuff, access your devices and network, and dig into the nooks and crannies of your machine. You can do a lot to customize this fabulous feature including adding and removing items of your choice from the sidebar, customizing the view options, and more.

Clean Up the Icons

If you find that you tend to view folders and files in Icon view, you have a handy cleanup option at your disposal in the Action menu in your Finder. You can apply this to any window that has lots of icons that need a bit of tidying up. Open your Finder and select a window with icons. Click the Action icon and select Clean Up By, and then choose Name, Kind, Date Modified, and so on to organize the icons in that window, as shown in the illustration. Your icons will be automatically organized into an evenly spaced grid.

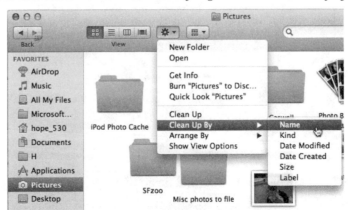

Add Items to the Sidebar

You can customize your sidebar by adding things you use most frequently, like a high-priority work folder, a favorite bit of software, or anything else you want to access quickly. If you are using an earlier version of OS X, Favorites will be analogous to Places in your OS X. The items you drag to the sidebar are not the actual items themselves but just shortcuts to these favorite items.

To add a new icon to your sidebar, simply drag the selected item from another window or from the desktop and into the sidebar under Favorites. Check that you see a little blue line before you release the file or folder, as shown in Figure 4-5.

Caution If you release the file or folder on a sidebar icon without seeing the blue line, the folder will be placed within that sidebar folder (rather than in the sidebar).

You can remove items from the sidebar by holding the COMMAND key and dragging the icon out of the sidebar. You'll see a little cloud when you do this, and when you release the item, the icon will disappear from your sidebar. It will still be in its original application, document, or folder.

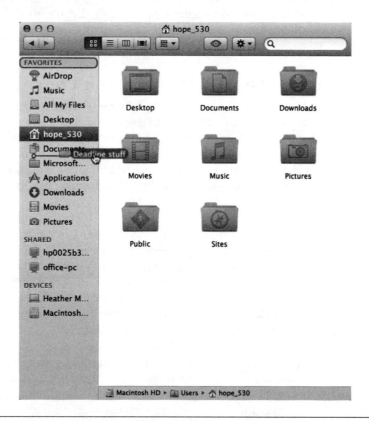

FIGURE 4-5   Drag an important file or folder to the Favorites section of the sidebar to see it each time you open your Finder.

Finally, you can also alter what you want to see in your Finder sidebar via the Finder Preferences pane. To do this, go to the Finder menu and select Preferences. You'll find your Finder menu by clicking once on the desktop. When you get to the Finder Preferences, click Sidebar and select or deselect the display options for your Finder, as shown here.

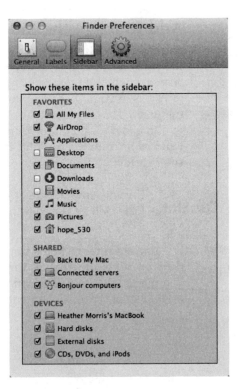

Tip   Have you misplaced your sidebar or toolbar? Sometimes when customizing your windows, you inadvertently "lose" a feature you didn't mean to. Also, if you accidentally hide the toolbar, your sidebar will disappear as well. There are Hide and Show options in the Finder menu where you can manage these features. Open Finder, click View from the menu, and select Show Sidebar or Show Toolbar as applicable.

Make Folders Open in the View You Prefer

You have a number of view options for your Finder windows including Icon view, List view, Column view, and Cover Flow view. If you find yourself constantly clicking to change the view options while in your Finder windows to get the "right" view, set the windows to open with the view option of your choice. You can decide to have documents or applications in List view and picture or movies in Icon view, for instance, or you may work best with total window uniformity. To configure a window to display in Icon view:

1. Launch Finder from the Dock and select an item in your sidebar.
2. Click View in the Finder menu and select View as Icons.
3. Click the Finder menu again and select Show View Options.
4. Check the box next to Always open in icon view (see Figure 4-6).
5. Use the sliders to increase or reduce the icon size and set the grid spacing (watch the window while you do this to see if you like the changes).
6. Select a Text size for the icon labels if you want.

You can explore more features as well. For example, you can also add a color background to your window by selecting Color and then selecting a color option. This is a useful tool to pick out a particular window when you need it. Finally, you can use a favorite picture as your window background. Select Picture and then drag an image from an open window and into the window you want to customize.

FIGURE 4-6   Set a window to always open in Icon view.

Note   If you click the Use as Defaults button, the view options you select for the window (in this case, the Pictures window) will be applied to all windows. So, if you created large icons or added a background picture, those settings will show up in every Finder window.

If you find that you want to view a particular window in List view, you have similar options for doing this. Once you have a folder selected in your Finder, go to the Finder menu and select List view. Go to the menu and click View, and then select Show View Options. For List view, you can customize the icon size and text size for that window, as well as show columns with information that is relevant to you, like Data Modified, Size, and so on, by selecting the appropriate box.

Note   You can increase the size of the font in the Finder sidebar, but you can't change the font type in the Finder or elsewhere on your Mac in Lion and Mountain Lion as you could in previous operating systems.

Customize the Finder Toolbar with Buttons You Use Most

You can add items to your Finder toolbar that you use frequently or delete those you don't use. For example, you may want to add the Label option to color-code your files and folders, or add the Eject icon if you frequently use discs on your Mac.

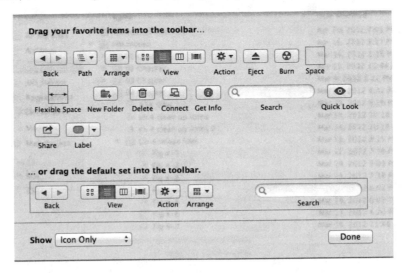

Once you make these changes, they will be applied to all of your Finder windows. To customize your toolbar, open Finder and do the following:

1. With Finder open, go to the menu and select View, then Customize Toolbar.
2. Click and drag a toolbar item (Delete, Label, and so on) to the Finder window and release when you see a green + (plus) symbol.
3. Click Done after you've added the items you want.

Tip You can select Icon and Text from the Show menu to display both the item's icon and a description. If you are new to OS X or your Mac, this is a good way to learn about these functions.

Configure Dashboard with Widgets You Use

Your dashboard contains smaller applications called widgets. *Widgets* perform simple tasks for you (calculator, clock, weather status) and also relate to your Mac applications like Calendar and Contacts (previously iCal and Address Book)—you can quickly check your daily schedule or look up a phone number or address. If you are in search of information or inspiration, you can download a widget to follow a blog, podcast, or news feed, look up a dinner recipe, or plan a vacation. It almost goes without saying that there are widgets available for fun—or procrastination—like Daily Factoid, Boredom Button, and a few hundred games. Launch your Dashboard in any of the following ways:

- Click the icon in the Dock.
- Use a three-finger sideways swipe to the left on your trackpad.
- Press the Dashboard key (F4) on your MacBook (if you have a more recent MacBook).
- Press FN-F12 on the keyboard

Add or Remove Widgets

Launch the Dashboard from your Dock—or whatever way works best for you. To add a widget to your Dashboard, click the plus (+) symbol in the lower-left corner of the screen. You'll be taken to a separate screen with a selection of different widgets as shown here. Click a widget icon once to add it to your Dashboard. If you don't see a widget you want to add, click More Widgets in the lower-left corner of the screen. You'll be taken to the Apple site for Dashboard widgets, where you can select from hundreds of widgets.

To remove a widget, launch Dashboard and click the minus (–) symbol in the lower-left corner of the screen. A letter x in a black circle appears in the upper-left corner of the widget. Click the x once to remove the widget.

Configure Widgets

Some widgets have a small "i" button in the lower-right corner that allows you to customize them. To determine whether you can configure a widget, hover your cursor in the lower-right corner of the widget and if an "i" appears, you can customize it. Click the "i" to enter your information (your location, language, and so on), as shown here in the weather widget.

Organize Apps in Launchpad

Launchpad is the central element of your OS X, which can get terribly crowded with icons, but you can quickly tidy it up to suit how you work. Apps are automatically organized first by the Apple apps that came with your OS X, usually taking up most of the first screen, and then any other apps that you download subsequently. You can move the icons around the screen, create more screens, or file apps together in a folder to keep your Launchpad organized and easy to use.

Arrange Apps Intuitively

You can move apps around Launchpad in any order that makes sense to you. Do this by clicking and dragging each one to a different location on the screen. The other icons will automatically adjust position when you drop the newly positioned icon. If you want, you can also create another Launchpad screen to view and organize the application icons. Create a new screen by clicking and dragging an icon to the right edge of the screen, much as you do on an iPhone or iPad, and the icon will be dropped into a new screen. From there, swipe between screens with two fingers and click and drag the app icons into the new screen.

Organize Apps in Folders

Another organizational tool at your disposal is to create folders on your Launchpad screen to file-related apps. For example, if you have a number of image editing programs, consider moving them into a folder and naming it "Image Editing." You might also want to arrange apps by how you use them, "time wasters" or "productivity apps," and so forth. How you arrange and label them is up to you. When you do create a folder, a name suggestion will be automatically assigned to the folder. You can change this name or leave it if it makes sense.

To create a folder:

1. Identify two apps that you want to file in the same folder.
2. Drag one app on top of the other and release it.
3. Select other apps that you want to include in the folder by repeating Steps 1 and 2.
4. Change the name of the folder if you want by highlighting the label and typing over it.

Personalize Mission Control

As you learned in the last chapter, Mission Control lets you see the Dashboard, all of the programs that are running, all of their open windows, and up to 16 Spaces, which function like virtual monitors or desktops—all in one bird's-eye view. If you have an application opened in full-screen view, you will see that application in Mission Control in one of the Spaces running along the top of the screen. You can add or delete Spaces, move a document or application into a Space, and customize other features in Mission Control in a way that makes sense to you.

Full-Screen Apps

One new and notable feature of Lion OS X was the addition of the full-screen app function. Applications like Mail, Calendar, Safari, FaceTime, and all of the apps in the iLife suite (GarageBand, iPhoto, iMovie) can be viewed in full-screen mode. You activate full-screen mode when the application is active by clicking a double arrow in the upper-right corner of the app. While you're in this mode, you won't see your main menu or your Dock—you see only a full-screen version of the application you're working with. When you go to Mission Control, each full-screen app you have opened will have its own space at the top of the Mission Control screen. To switch back to a regular window, point your cursor at the upper-right corner until a blue version of the double arrows appears, and click that to reduce the window.

Create Multiple Desktops

You can create multiple desktops and add a specific document or application to that Space. This goes a long way toward keeping each one free of clutter and easy to navigate. Each desktop will still have any items you left on your first desktop as well as the Dock. To create a new desktop Space, launch Mission Control and move your cursor to the upper-right corner of the screen. When the plus (+) sign appears, click it to add a desktop to the top of Mission Control, as shown in Figure 4-7. Finally, drag a window or application onto the new desktop Space. To switch between the desktops while you work, use a three-finger swipe right or left on your trackpad to flip through each one.

FIGURE 4-7 Add a new desktop to Spaces at the top of your Mission Control screen.

 Tip You can also drag a window or an entire application to the top-right corner of the Mission Control screen, and OS X will automatically create a new Space for the window or application.

To delete a desktop, point your cursor at it and wait until a black x symbol appears. Click the x symbol to remove the desktop from Mission Control.

Create Keyboard Shortcuts for Multiple Desktops

If you don't have a trackpad, you can configure shortcuts to get to each desktop. To set up shortcuts for navigating through multiple desktops:

1. Go to System Preferences, select Keyboard, and then click the Keyboard Shortcuts tab at the top of the window.
2. Select Mission Control from the list on the left.

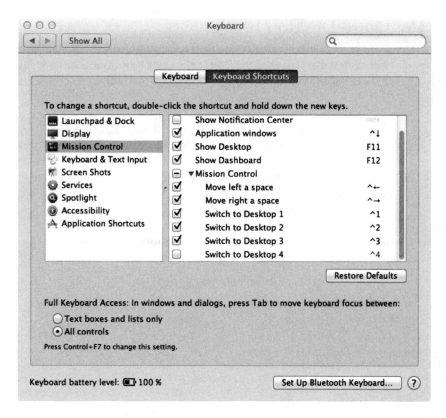

3. Select the check boxes next to each of the shortcuts you want to enable. These are shown as Desktop 1, Desktop 2, and so on.
4. Close the Keyboard Preferences pane.

After selecting these options, you can navigate through each of your desktops by pressing CONTROL and typing the desktop number. To move right or left one space, press CONTROL and the left or right arrow key.

Move Desktops Around

If multiple full-screen apps are opened and you have a number of desktops created, you can rearrange them into any order you want. For example, you may want to have your Mail desktop as the first you flip through, or put them in some other order. Start Mission Control and click and drag the desktop icons horizontally across the top of the screen to rearrange their order.

Configure Desktop Images

Unless you change them, each of the desktop backgrounds will display the image you selected for your first desktop. You can add different desktop displays to each of your desktops to help differentiate them from each other. To configure different desktop images:

1. Click System Preferences and select Desktop & Screen Saver.
2. Launch Mission Control and drag the Preferences window to the desktop you want to customize.
3. Click the Desktop Preferences pane and select a desktop image for that desktop.
4. Launch Mission Control, drag the Preferences window to the next desktop, and repeat the process in Step 3.

When you are finished, you will have several distinct, individualized desktops to flip through at your convenience.

5 Optimize iTunes

This chapter outlines strategies to optimize your iTunes application on your Mac and to share media over your network and devices. Program optimization is simply the process of making a software application work more efficiently or more quickly. In the case of iTunes, the sheer volume of files most of us collect can interfere with the ease and efficiency of using the application. You don't have to be a programmer to make a favorite application work the way you want, though. In iTunes there are several steps you can take to ensure that you spend less time searching for your files and more time enjoying the music and media in your library.

Note The tips in this chapter assume that you have a collection of media in your library already, whether ripped CDs, music from the iTunes Store, or apps for your iOS devices. If you don't have a lot of media in your library yet, you can use the suggestions to help you keep iTunes optimized as your library grows.

Explore iTunes Preferences

Customizing the preferences in iTunes can help you better locate and use the media you want. As you probably know, there are several ways to view content in your library, but two options that are most useful for managing larger libraries are explored next, including organizing your content in List view and Album List view. Within these options there are a number of preferences you can enable to customize your view and sort through your media efficiently.

Configure the Column Browser

The Column Browser is an effective tool for navigating through the media in your library, and is especially useful if your library has grown to unruly proportions. When you enable the Column Browser, you can quickly sort through your media files to find just what you want. You choose how you want the Column Browser to display by selecting from a number of options about the type of information you want to display and also where the Column Browser displays in your library. To use the Column Browser, press COMMAND-B or click the View menu and select Column Browser, and then do the following:

1. Go to the View menu, select Column Browser, and then select the options you want to display in the submenu. You have up to five choices: Genres, Artists, Albums, Composers, and Groupings.
2. Select how you want to display the column browser, On Top or On Left.

If you want to use the Column Browser in your other libraries, say Movies or Podcasts, you have to enable it while you're in those libraries. The selection you make in Music will only apply to that library.

Note   If you set the Column Browser to display on the left and then choose more than one option to display (for example, Genres, Artists, and Albums), this feature will take up a lot of your display space. It's fine to display this on the left if you prefer and don't mind scrolling to the right to view your content. However, for most of us with smaller screens, the top of the library is the best position for the Column Browser.

Remove Items from the Source List

The Source List is the column on the left of your iTunes library and contains links to each of your libraries as well as links to the Store, your devices, and Playlists.

You can remove library items that you might not use, like Podcasts, Ping, or Radio. Eliminate clutter from your application by removing the items you don't use, by doing the following:

1. Click the iTunes menu and select General Preferences.
2. Check that you have the General tab selected at the top of the Preferences pane.
3. Clear the check boxes next to the features of the library that you never use.
4. Click OK.

Optimize the iTunes Libraries

You can optimize your libraries (Music, Movies, Podcasts) by deleting files you don't want and making the most of the files you do want. You may have duplicates of music or possibly old podcasts clogging up your library, which need to be removed. If you ripped your CDs into your music library, you may have missing track information or artwork. This section will outline some of the ways you can optimize the contents in your library by keeping file sizes small while importing, adding information you're missing, deleting information you don't want, and adding tags to help your organize your library and help you create great playlists.

Choose Import Settings That Save Space

Whether you have a full to overflowing library or are still building your iTunes collection, there are ways to import music but still save on disk space. When you rip CDs to your library, iTunes imports the files encoded in AAC by default. To do this, the digital file is compressed and some of the data is actually removed. The sound quality is reduced, but not so much that the average listener notices. In fact, all the music you download from iTunes is encoded in AAC by default. If saving space is the highest priority, then confirm that you have the default AAC encoder selected in iTunes Preferences. There may be times when you want to encode a file in a different format to preserve the highest sound quality or when you want to burn the files to a disc. To determine the best configuration for you, do the following in iTunes and review the pros and cons of each setting:

1. Open iTunes and press COMMAND-comma, or click the iTunes menu and select Preferences.
2. Check that you are in the General Preferences pane and click Import Settings.
3. Click the pop-up menu next to Import Using and select from one of these options:
   - **AAC Encoder**   Music files encoded in AAC are compressed, which makes them smaller but also reduces the sound quality somewhat. Most listeners won't notice a difference between an original CD track and one encoded in AAC. If you want to save space, keep the AAC Encoder selected in Import Settings Preferences.

- **AIFF Encoder**   Files encoded in AIFF aren't compressed and will take up much more space compared with other import options. If you want the very best music quality or want to burn the music back to a CD for some reason, you would use AIFF or WAV. For everyday listening on your iPod, a compressed file works better.
- **Apple Lossless Encoder**   Some compression occurs when music files are encoded in Apple Lossless format, but the sound quality is better than AAC and MP3 formats. The drawback to encoding your music in this format is that you get a larger file size (though still smaller than either an AIFF or WAV file). Files encoded in Apple Lossless sound better when burned to CD than AAC or MP3 files but not as high-quality as AIFF or WAV.
- **MP3 Encoder**   As with AAC, encoding a file in MP3 will remove some of the audio data to compress the file. The file size is similar to that of an AAC file but the quality may be slightly less. However, MP3 files can be played on a wider variety of players and applications.
- **WAV Encoder**   Files aren't compressed when encoded in WAV and will take up a huge amount of space. The sound quality will be comparable to that of your CD, but you will lose lots of space in the process and will be unable to add as many tracks to your iPod as you would with a compressed file type.

After you select your option from the pop-up menu, click OK. Remember that music downloaded from iTunes will already be encoded in AAC and you can't change the format to a higher-quality encoding like Apple Lossless or WAV.

Locate and Delete Duplicate Data

After you amass a collection of library contents by ripping CDs, or buying music from the iTunes Store and elsewhere, it's not unusual to find that you've added some items to your library more than once. It's easy to get rid of duplicates, and your iTunes application comes with a built-in search tool to help you identify duplicates. To locate any duplicates in your library:

1. Click Music or another section of your library.
2. Go to the File menu and select Display Duplicates.
3. Sort the list by date to show the most recently added media.

4. Select the item or items you want to delete, click the Edit menu, and select Delete.

If you have slightly different versions of the same song by the same artist, say a live or acoustic version and a studio recording, they will display as duplicates even though they are actually different and you probably want to keep both. You can do a search for exact duplicates if your duplicates list is very long. Hold down the OPTION key, click File, and then select Show Exact Duplicates.

Get Missing Cover Art

If you added music to your library via your CD collection, you probably can't see the cover art that goes with the original album. This isn't a huge problem, but it's handy to have the visual of the album in question when playing and organizing your library.

iTunes has a search feature that helps you locate missing cover art; you just need to be connected to the Internet for this to work. To add missing cover art to the tracks and albums in your Music library through iTunes, do the following:

1. Go to Advanced in the menu.
2. Select Get Album Artwork and confirm that you want to do this by clicking the default button in the dialog box that appears.
3. Wait while iTunes locates and loads the artwork.

You can also set up iTunes to look for missing art automatically. Go to Preferences in the menu and click the General tab. Select the check box for Automatically download missing album artwork. Each time you load music into your library from another source, iTunes will search for the artwork for you.

Add Cover Art to Your Library Manually

You can manually add cover art to your library that you don't find by using iTunes search. You can use images you find on the Internet, scan a CD cover, or use some other image of your choosing to serve as the cover art. Look for album artwork on sites like Wikipedia or Amazon. When you find an image file, save it by right-clicking or CONTROL-clicking it and selecting the Save As option to save it to your hard drive. Then do the following to add the artwork to a single track:

1. Select the song by clicking it once.
2. Select File and Get Info or press COMMAND-I.
3. Click the Artwork tab and click Add (see Figure 5-1).
4. Find the image on your computer and double-click it.
5. Click OK to add the artwork to your song file.

Tip You can also drag artwork to a single track while in List view by dragging it to the lower-left corner of your iTunes library in the Now Playing window.

To add artwork to an entire album, do the following:

1. Select View as Grid from the menu.
2. Click the album cover to select it and select File/Get Info or press COMMAND-I. You can also select View as Grid and click the album outline to select the whole album.

FIGURE 5-1   Add cover art to a music track in your iTunes library.

3. Click Yes when a screen appears asking: "Are you sure you want to edit information for multiple items?"
4. Select the check box next to Artwork.
5. Open a Finder window that contains the album artwork and drag it into the artwork box. Release the image when you see a green plus + symbol.
6. Click OK.

Fix Incorrect Information

You can use a number of sources to download your media to iTunes, but not all of them contain the correct information for the media you have. Also, if you download a single track from an album and then download other tracks at a later date, the track numbering can sometimes be out of sequence. You can change the information in your library by changing the tags in the Information pane. Tags include things like the track name, artist, year, album, and genre. (The information for other media in your library, like podcasts, will have different tags.)

To fix the incorrect information for a single track or album:

1. Select a track or tracks to edit.
2. Click the File menu and select Get Info or press COMMAND-I.
3. Click the Info tab to view the information for that track.
4. Type over the incorrect information and add any additional information to the track. You can change only one track at a time.
5. Click OK when you are done.

You can't edit track information when you select more than one track at a time. To edit the track sequence, select one track at a time and enter the listing for the individual track.

Add Tags to Your Library Content

Adding tags to your content helps you find and organize your media and makes it easy to create great playlists. Some tags are already included in music or other media that you have in your library, but you can customize this information in a way that is most useful to you. You can come up with a new genre tag for a collection of music you have. For example, if you have a very large collection of jazz music, you can create subgenres like Early Jazz or Smooth Jazz, and include information about the year the music was created. With this kind of additional information, you can quickly create specialized jazz playlists based on the subgenre you create or the year the music was recorded. You can apply ratings to your music, up to five stars for each song, as well as expand on a range of information about the content.

In addition to editing information about name, artist, and track, here is a summary of additional tags you can include:

- **Year**   Add information about when the recording or film was made or when a piece of music was performed, depending on your preference.
- **Album Artist**   Add additional artist information to the track or album if more than one artist performs. For example, on a compilation of Ella Fitzgerald songs, if one song is a duet with Louis Armstrong, you can add his name to the track.
- **Composer**   Include information about the composer or songwriter. This is especially handy for classical music albums.
- **Comments**   Add any information here that will help you organize your music; for example, whether it's an acoustic or live version of a song.
- **Genre**   Include customized genre information to your tracks. You can select from existing tags on the pop-up menu or create your own customized genre information.
- **Sort Tags**   *Sort tags* are specialized tags that allow you to work around how tracks are sorted in iTunes by default. For example, if you have tracks by multiple artists, but want them sorted by one main artist, you can configure the tracks to display by that artist name only. Or if you have a large collection of classical music, you can include sort tags to sort the music by the composer's name rather than the conductor. All the other tag information is retained and displayed when you use sort tags.

To change the information on a track:

1. Select a track or a selection of tracks to edit.
2. Press COMMAND-I or click the File menu and select Get Info. Note that if you select more than one track, you must confirm that you want to edit multiple items, and you will get an Info pane showing that you are editing multiple items.

3. Check that the Info tab is selected at the top, and then edit the information for Artist, Year, Composer, and so on as applicable.

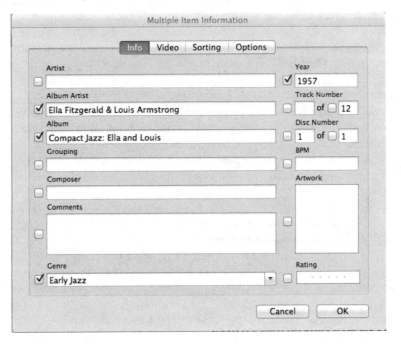

4. Select a different genre from the pop-up list or enter your own genre by selecting and typing over the genre name.
5. To edit your sort tags, click the Sorting tab at the top of the Information pane. To change how the track sorts, enter information into the right side of the pane under Sort Name, Sort Artist, and so on (the current sort defaults are highlighted on the left side of the pane). If you want to sort by a composer's name, for example, enter the name under Sort Composer on the right of the pane. The original tags will be retained and displayed but the way the track will sort differs.
6. When you have finished adding tags to your files, click OK.

Tip   Select the yes check box for compilations if the tracks you are tagging are part of a compilation. For example, if you have a "Best of the 80s" album that you copied to your library, each track will show up as a separate album and artist unless you select this option. A compilation CD may have a dozen or more artists and songs, so you can tell iTunes to keep them together by selecting this check box. However, if the compilation is by a single artist, don't select the Part of a Compilation check box.

Finally, you can add or change the star ratings of your albums or tracks by clicking in the ratings column and selecting the number of stars you want to assign to them. This is another tag that helps you sort your music and create playlists with your favorite music.

Create Useful Smart Playlists

Smart playlists are a great way to enjoy the content in your library. Most of us have so many albums and tracks that a simple shuffle on our iPods means we'll never get to listen to all the music. iTunes already has smart playlists configured for you; just look in the lower-left side of the Source List and note My Top Rated, Recently Added, and Top 25 Most Played. You can create your own playlist based on genre and also add other rules to narrow the selection even further. For example, you can select Rock genre but only include what you added recently, or you can exclude certain artists from the playlist (see Figure 5-2).

To create a smart playlist with rules:

1. Select New Smart Playlist from the File menu.
2. Click the pop-up menu and select an option from the list (Genre in the example shown in Figure 5-2).
3. Select an option from the second pop-up menu. The options will vary depending on the selection you made in the first pop-up menu. For Genre, you are given the choice of Contains/does not contain, Is/is not, Begins with/ends with.
4. Enter a term in the third field (Rock, Classical, and so on.).
5. Click the plus symbol to create an additional rule if you want.
6. Limit the playlist to 25 items or a number of your choice by entering it in the box next to Limit to.
7. Verify that "Match all of the following rules" is checked at the top and click OK.

You can change or edit the rules in your smart playlist once you create it by clicking the playlist, selecting File, and then clicking Edit Smart Playlist. You can add, remove, or change any of the rules or create a bigger playlist by entering a larger number.

FIGURE 5-2 Create a Smart Playlist based on genre, recent additions to your library, and more. You can also tell iTunes exactly how many tracks you want to include on the playlist.

If you hold down the OPTION key while you are in the Smart Playlist dialog box, an ellipsis displays instead of the + button. When you click the ellipsis, you can add a subrule to the rule immediately above it.

Get Rid of Unwanted Playlists

After you listen to a certain playlist a few times, you may find you are no longer interested in it or want to make room for new playlists. Fortunately, deleting playlists is simple. Select the playlist in the Source List and click Delete.

Create Playlist Folders

Depending on how many playlists you create and want to keep, you may want to create folders for your playlists to keep them organized and to avoid having to scroll up and down in the Source List to find what you want. You can organize them by category depending on when you listen to them; for example, commute playlist, kids' tunes, and so on. Do the following to move your playlists into folders:

1. Go to the File menu and select New Playlist Folder.
2. Enter a name by typing over the default folder name.
3. Click and drag your playlists in the Source List to the new folder. Once you do this, a drop-down arrow will appear next to the folder. You can hide and show the contents of the playlist folder by clicking the arrow.

Set Old Podcasts to Delete Automatically

If you are a fan of podcasts and have subscribed to several, you may find that you have a number of old podcasts filling up your library. You can identify which podcasts you haven't listened to by looking at the left side of your podcast list. If there is a blue dot next to the podcast, it's new and you haven't listened to it. The absence of a blue dot indicates that it's a podcast you have listened to (a half dot is a podcast you partially listened to). If you find that you have lots of old podcasts in your iTunes library, you may need to change your settings to automatically delete podcasts based on criteria you set. To set your podcasts to delete automatically:

1. Click Podcasts in the Source List of iTunes.
2. Click Settings beneath the list of podcasts.
3. Click the pop-up menu next to Episodes to keep, and select an option (all unplayed episodes, two episodes, ten episodes, and so on.)
4. Click OK when you are done.

If you choose to keep all unplayed episodes, any episodes that you have played will automatically disappear from your iTunes library.

Optimize Connected Devices

When you're not using your Mac, your iOS devices are the best way to listen to your music, watch programs, or use all the cool apps you buy from the iTunes Store and elsewhere. Optimizing your devices is as important as keeping your libraries organized and free of clutter. As your library grows, you need to come up with new strategies to manage and sync your media collection.

Delete Unwanted Data from iDevices

You probably have a good idea about exactly how much music you have on your device, as most people very deliberately sync what they want to their devices so they can enjoy their music away from their computer. Something that can sneak up on you is the number of apps you have. It's easy to download apps while browsing in Safari, or perhaps a sneaky child downloaded an app while borrowing your device. Apps can be big storage hogs, so looking for candidates to delete can save you space on your device if you are running low. You can quickly assess just how many apps you have and exactly how much space they are using by sorting through your iTunes library.

1. Click the Apps library from your Source List.
2. Select List View and click the Size column to sort your apps by size. Take note especially of the larger items at the top of the list that you don't use. Sort by other criteria (name, date of download, and so on) if you want.
3. Select an item you want to delete and press Delete on the keyboard. Confirm that you want to delete the item when prompted.

Follow the same steps for any other data in your library that you want to delete, like Movies, TV Shows, or Podcasts, if you think there may be a lot of unwanted data there.

If you prefer to work directly from your iOS 5 device, you can do the following to view how much room your data is taking up and also to remove it from your device:

1. Tap the Settings icon on your iOS device.
2. Go to General and select Usage. On an iPad you tap Usage and then Manage Storage. The first items on the list are Video and Music, but as you scroll down, you see information about app usage and how much space each app is taking up on your device.
3. Scroll down and tap Show all Apps to display the entire list of the apps on your device. Note they are displayed from the biggest size to the smallest.
4. Tap on an app you want to delete and tap the red Delete App button.
5. If you have a lot of video content or unwanted music on your iOS device, you can follow the same steps to delete them directly from your device.

Note These steps only work for devices that run iOS 5. For an older iOS, you can manage the data you want to delete directly in the iTunes library.

You can reinstall apps you purchased through the iTunes Store if you later decide you want them after all. Any information stored within the apps will no longer be there (your scores on a video game, for example), but you can start anew by clicking the Purchased link in your Source List. Once you click Purchased, click the Download Previous Purchases link from the lower-right corner of your library, and your older purchases will be added to your library once again.

Revisit Syncing Configurations

Even if you delete unwanted data from your iTunes library or iOS device, you may still find that you don't have enough room on your device to sync your entire library. If your syncing is configured to automatically sync everything in your library, you may have even seen a message warning you that you don't have enough room on your device. If you have the room, it's easiest to sync everything, but if you don't, you need to come up with a new approach to syncing. You can decide what to sync to your device and what to keep in your library. Perhaps you only want music on your iPod and prefer to use apps on your iPad.

Sync Selected Items Automatically

If your library is too big to fit on your device, you can choose to sync only your favorite music or playlists, podcasts, and essential apps automatically with your device. Do the following to configure the content you want to include when you sync your device to your library. This example is for the Music library, but you can apply the same steps to your Movies, TV Shows, Podcasts, and Apps.

1. Open iTunes and connect your iOS device.
2. Click the device in the Source List.
3. When the Summary page displays, scroll down to the bottom of your library to Options and select the check box next to Sync only checked songs and videos.
4. Click the Music tab at the top of the summary page to select the music you want to sync with your device.
5. Select the button next to Selected playlists, artists, albums and genres (see Figure 5-3). Choose whether you want to include music videos and voice memos as part of your sync.
6. Select the check box next to Automatically fill free space with songs if you think you may have space left over after syncing.
7. Scroll through the Playlists, Artists, Genres, and Albums lists and select the check boxes next to the content you want to sync with your device.
8. Click Apply after you select the music items you want to sync.

Tip   Watch the Capacity bar at the bottom of the library when you are considering what items to add. You may have more room than you think.

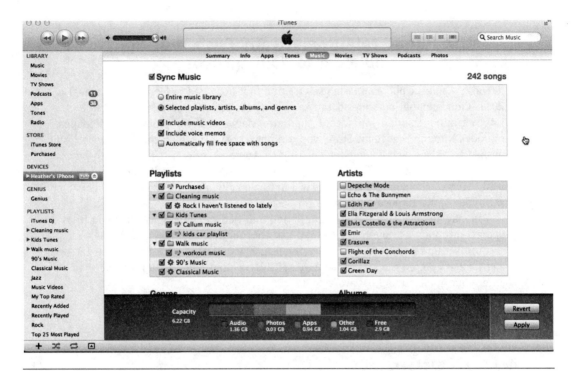

FIGURE 5-3 Select the specific playlists, artists, albums, and genres you want to sync to your device rather than your whole library.

You can sync select apps in much the same way. You can also have your newly purchased apps automatically pushed to your devices with iCloud. See the "Use iCloud to Automatically Push Your Apps and More to Your Devices" sidebar for more information on how to configure this. To select the apps you want on your device, follow Steps 1 to 3 described previously and then do the following:

1. Click the Apps tab at the top of the iTunes library.
2. Select the Sync Apps check box if it isn't already selected.
3. Scroll through and check the apps you want on your device, as shown here.
4. Click Apply when you finish to begin the sync of your selected apps.
5. Press COMMAND-E or go to the Controls menu and select Eject to remove your device from your computer.

Use iCloud to Automatically Push Your Apps and More to Your Devices

iCloud is Apple's cloud computing service and first appeared in Lion in the summer of 2011. Cloud computing stores data like your music and apps on remote servers on the Internet rather than on your local computer or network. If you purchase music, apps, or books through the iTunes Store, you can opt to have those purchases automatically pushed to all the devices registered with your Apple ID, effectively syncing these new items directly to your devices. It doesn't matter if you bought an item on your iPhone, iPod, iPad, or computer; these items will automatically go to all the devices registered with your Apple ID once you enable this option.

You may already have iCloud set up if you followed the directions when you first upgraded to Lion or Mountain Lion. You can confirm that you have your iCloud account set up by going to System Preferences and selecting iCloud under the Internet and Wireless preferences, as shown next. If the account is not set up, you need to enter your Apple ID and password to do so.

To enable automatic push of new purchases to your iTunes library on your Mac:

1. Open iTunes.
2. Select Preferences from the iTunes menu or press COMMAND-comma.
3. Click the Store tab at the top of the Preferences pane.
4. Check the boxes next to the items you want to automatically push to your devices (for example, Music, Apps, or Books).
5. Click OK to apply the push settings.

To enable automatic push of new purchases made on other devices:

1. Tap the Settings icon from your Home screen.
2. Tap Store.
3. Select the items you want to push by moving the slidebars to the ON position. You can choose Music or Apps for your iPhone or iPod touch and Music, Apps, and Books for your iPad.

Note   iOS 5 is only compatible with the following devices: iPhone 3GS, iPhone 4, iPhone 4S, iPod touch 3rd and 4th Generation, and all the iPad devices to date. If you have an older device, you won't be able to run iOS 5 on your device or use the iCloud push option.

Sync Your Devices Wirelessly

You can sync your media without a USB cable if you set this up in your iTunes library. First connect your iOS 5 device with a USB and sync it as you normally do. After the sync is complete, do the following to set up wireless syncing:

1. Check that the device is selected in the Source List.
2. On the Summary page in iTunes, scroll down to the Options section at the bottom of the library.
3. Select the check box next to Sync with this iPod (or iPad or iPhone) over Wi-Fi.
4. Click Apply.

After you set your devices up to sync wirelessly, they will automatically appear under the Devices section of your Source List. You can sync your content either through your iTunes library or directly from your device. To sync from your library, click the device in the Source List and sync as you do normally. If you want to sync from your device, do the following:

1. Tap the Settings icon on your device and select General.
2. Tap iTunes Wi-Fi Sync.
3. Tap the Sync Now button and wait while your content syncs.
4. If you decide later that you prefer the USB sync method, simply clear the check box next to Sync over Wi-Fi in the Options section of your library.

Share Your Media on a Network

You can make your iTunes library available to other computers in your house through Home Sharing or other iTunes users over a shared network. With either of these options enabled, other users can access the music, video, and other content in your library and stream it directly to their Mac or PC. If the other user configures their libraries to do the same, you can access their content as well. You can also share content between user accounts on the same computer. This can be especially useful if you have different devices and different opinions about what you want to use from a shared library and how you want to sync the media. To get started with sharing your media, you need to have a wireless connection and an Apple ID.

 Sharing media is not the same as copying it from one Apple ID account to another, which is a violation of copyrighted materials. Sharing across a network allows others to stream the content on their computers and enjoy it in much the same way as if they came to your home and listened to a CD or watched a film from your collection.

Share Media with Other Computers in Your Home

With Home Sharing, you can move and copy songs from one computer to another—provided you use the same Apple ID account on each computer. You can authorize up to five different computers with your account, including PCs. To enable home sharing:

1. Click the Advanced menu in iTunes and select Turn on Home Sharing.
2. Type your Apple ID in the box and enter your password.

3. Click the Create Home Share button. You may see a message "Home Sharing could not be activated because this computer is not authorized for the account 'john@mail.com.' Would you like to authorize now?" Click the Authorize button to continue.
4. Click Done when you get a confirmation screen saying that Home Sharing is on.

FIGURE 5-4 Copy music from other computers in your home with Home Sharing.

When Home Sharing is set up, you will see a library name under the Shared section of your Source List. Click the library to access the contents and play the music or stream videos on your computer (if the videos were purchased in iTunes). To copy files from the other library:

1. Check that you are in the other library by clicking it under Shared in the Source List.
2. Select the track or tracks you want to copy (see Figure 5-4).
3. Click the Import button and wait while iTunes imports the tracks to your computer.

When iTunes is done copying the music, you can add or edit the information in the files to help you include the new media in your playlists.

Share Your Library with Others on a Network

If you have different computers with separate Apple ID accounts on your network, you can enable sharing so that other users on other computers can stream content from your library. If they configure their computer to do the same, you can access and enjoy their content as long as you both have the share option enabled.

Note   You can't copy or move content from another user's library using this method because two different Apple ID accounts are involved.

To enable sharing from your Mac:

1. Select Preferences from the iTunes menu and click the Sharing tab.
2. Select Share my library on my local network.
3. Choose to share either your entire library or selected playlists by clicking the button next to either option. If you choose to share only selected playlists, go through the list and select the check box next to the items you want to share (see Figure 5-5).
4. Select Require password and enter a password.
5. If you want iTunes to update the play count for a song whenever it is played, select the check box at the bottom of the pane. If you want to count only the plays on your computer, leave this check box blank.
6. Click OK.

Caution   If you are on a public network at a library, coffee shop, or other location and open iTunes with the share option enabled, anyone on the same network can view the content in your iTunes library. Consider setting a password so that you share your media library only with other users you know and give the password to.

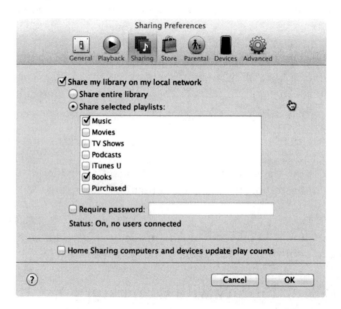

FIGURE 5-5   Choose what content you want to share over a network by opting to share only selected content.

To enable sharing from a PC:

1. Click the Edit menu and select Preferences.
2. Click the Sharing tab.
3. Select Share entire library or Share selected playlists. If you opt to share only selected playlists, select the check box next to the items you want to share.
4. Select Require a password and enter a password in the box.
5. Click OK.

Share Your iTunes Media Library with Account Users on Your Mac

If you have one Mac and a number of users with different devices, you can take advantage of User Accounts on your computer to share a library and allow each user to sync the media they want to their device. Even when users share the same Apple ID, each can configure their own playlists and sync what they want to their device. To share your iTunes Media library with other account users, you have to move the library to a public location on your computer (see Figure 5-6).

FIGURE 5-6   iTunes media folder in the Shared folder on your Mac HD. In this location, other account users on your Mac can access and copy the library content.

The following steps explain how to move the media library to the Shared folder in your Users folder, but you can also move it to the Public folder.

1. Quit iTunes.
2. Find your iTunes Media library folder on your computer; it's usually in the Music Folder or Documents. If you are having trouble locating it, do a quick search with Spotlight.
3. Move the iTunes Media folder to /Users/Shared on your Mac HD.
4. Open iTunes and choose Preferences from the iTunes menu or press COMMAND-comma. Click the Advanced tab in Preferences.
5. Click Change and navigate to the location of your iTunes Media folder, and then click Open when you confirm that your library is in the Shared folder.

Now that your library is in a shared location, each account user can log in and access iTunes from within their account. They can create their own playlists and sync the media they want to their devices. First, each user must open iTunes and add the media to the library in their account.

1. Open iTunes in a different account.
2. From the File menu, choose Add to Library.
3. In the window that opens, navigate to the Shared folder and click Open.

Note that all the media files in the library will be added to the other user account library, including apps, podcasts, movies, and other content. Depending on the size of the library, it may take several minutes to add to the other user account.

Back Up Your Library

The amount of energy, not to mention money, that goes into a decent iTunes library makes backing up the media a priority for most users. By far the best way to ensure that your media is backed up is to enable Time Machine, which regularly (and automatically) backs up all the content on your Mac, including your media library. You can learn how to set up Time Machine in Chapter 1 if you don't have it set up already.

If you prefer to back up your library manually to an external hard drive, you can do this in a few simple steps. First, locate your iTunes media library (in Music or Documents or in Shared if you moved it there to share your library). Next, locate your external hard drive, either in the Finder sidebar or on your desktop. Drag your iTunes media folder to the external hard drive and wait while it copies. It can take a while depending on the number of files you have.

6 Take Control of Mail

Email is such an integral part of how we communicate with others that it's difficult to imagine a time when we didn't have hundreds of messages to sort through each morning when we turn our computers on. Unfortunately, the success of email has created a new set of problems, as sorting out the good stuff from the junk can eat up a lot of valuable time. The Mail application on your Mac has many built-in tools to help you find the messages you want and get rid of those that you don't. This chapter will explore some of the ways you can use Mail to get rid of spam, organize contacts, and manage all those hundreds of daily messages.

Reduce Spam

Spam is an annoying reality of having an email account; whether it's a notice from a bank in some far-away country promising you millions (if only you'd provide your banking details) or advertisements from retailers you have no interest in buying from. Spam can also contain malicious attachments that can cause harm to your Mac. It is virtually impossible to eliminate spam from your inbox completely, but you can take steps to reduce and manage the amount of unsolicited mail you receive so that you can get to the important stuff in your inbox straight away.

Keep Your Email Address Quiet

Keeping an email address quiet doesn't mean keeping it from friends and family (unless of course, you want to). It means not using it in public Internet forums, to sign up for special offers with retailers, or otherwise enter it into any web form. Often the point of these endeavors is to allow spammers to collect email addresses and use them or sell them to people who send you the junk that is clogging up your mailboxes.

Some other tips to keep in mind:

- *Don't click a link in a suspicious mail that says "click here to remove."* This confirms to the spammers that the address they have for you is a legitimate, working email address.
- *Avoid using your email address on a personal blog or web page.* If you want to include a contact email, use an obfuscated one that can be read by the human eye.

- *Don't participate in forwarding any chain letters.* You know the ones; a friend will send a funny series of pictures or a compelling story and ask you to send it on to ten friends. Don't. These chain letters can easily fall into the hands of spammers, who will harvest the email addresses in the chain.
- *Create an email address that is hard to figure out.* Many spammers generate email addresses based on common first and surnames. The John Smiths of the world who use johnsmith@mail.com are inundated with spam emails. Use a nickname or some original combination of your name and letters to create a spam-resistant email address.

Beware of Phishing Scams

Phishing is one way that cyber criminals tap into your personal or financial information. A phishing email typically looks like an email from an organization or institution you have an account with, like your bank, PayPal, or a favorite online retailer or service provider. The following image shows a phishing email masquerading as a legitimate email from YouTube. Hover your cursor over the link (but don't click!), and note that the URL embedded in the note and the actual URL are different.

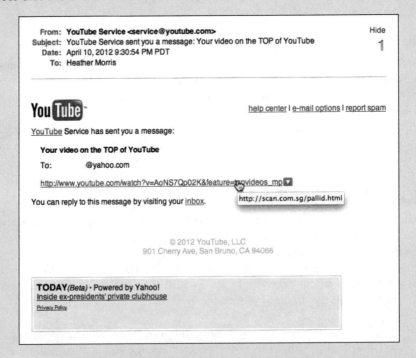

These seemingly legitimate emails will ask you to update your account information, change your password, or confirm some other piece of personal information like your social security number or PIN. It's important to know that banks and retailers will *never* ask you for this information in an email. If you receive an email that you think may be a phishing scam trying to get your personal information, keep the following in mind:

- Don't click any link in an email that you believe is a phishing scam no matter how convincing the email appears.
- If the email contains some sort of threat if you don't act (your account will be closed, you will be fined, and so on), you can be fairly certain it's not a legitimate email.
- Evaluate the claim that is being made in the email. Obvious scams are that you won a contest you didn't enter or that you are getting something for free, if only you click the link to find out.
- Preview the link in Mail by holding the cursor over it—but don't click. If the link that is embedded in the note doesn't match the URL you see in the preview (as in the YouTube example shown earlier), it isn't a legitimate link.
- If the email has a lot of spelling or grammar mistakes, it's probably from scammers. Most businesses invest a lot of time in getting their correspondence to customers just right.

If you are still in doubt about whether the email is legitimate, you can check with the company in question and either contact them by phone or log in to your (legitimate) account on their web site to check whether there are any alerts attached to your account or messages that need your immediate attention.

Have a Disposable Address

If you want to continue to use online forums, shop, and otherwise make your presence felt on the Web, consider creating a disposable email address for these activities. There are lots of mail providers to choose from, or you can create an additional account with your current provider. If the account becomes overrun with spam after a period of time, you can abandon it and sign up for another. Although there are many mail providers, there are only so many email addresses available, so consider creating an account with a lesser-known domain extension (that last part of the email address after the @ symbol). See Figure 6-1.

To get a free Yahoo! email account:

1. Open Safari and go to mail.yahoo.com.
2. Click the Create New Account tab at the bottom of the screen.
3. Enter your personal details including your name and location.
4. Enter an email name and select an alternate (suffix): ymail.com or rocketmail.com.
5. Select an ID and password and enter information for password clues.
6. Type in the visual code and click Create My Account.

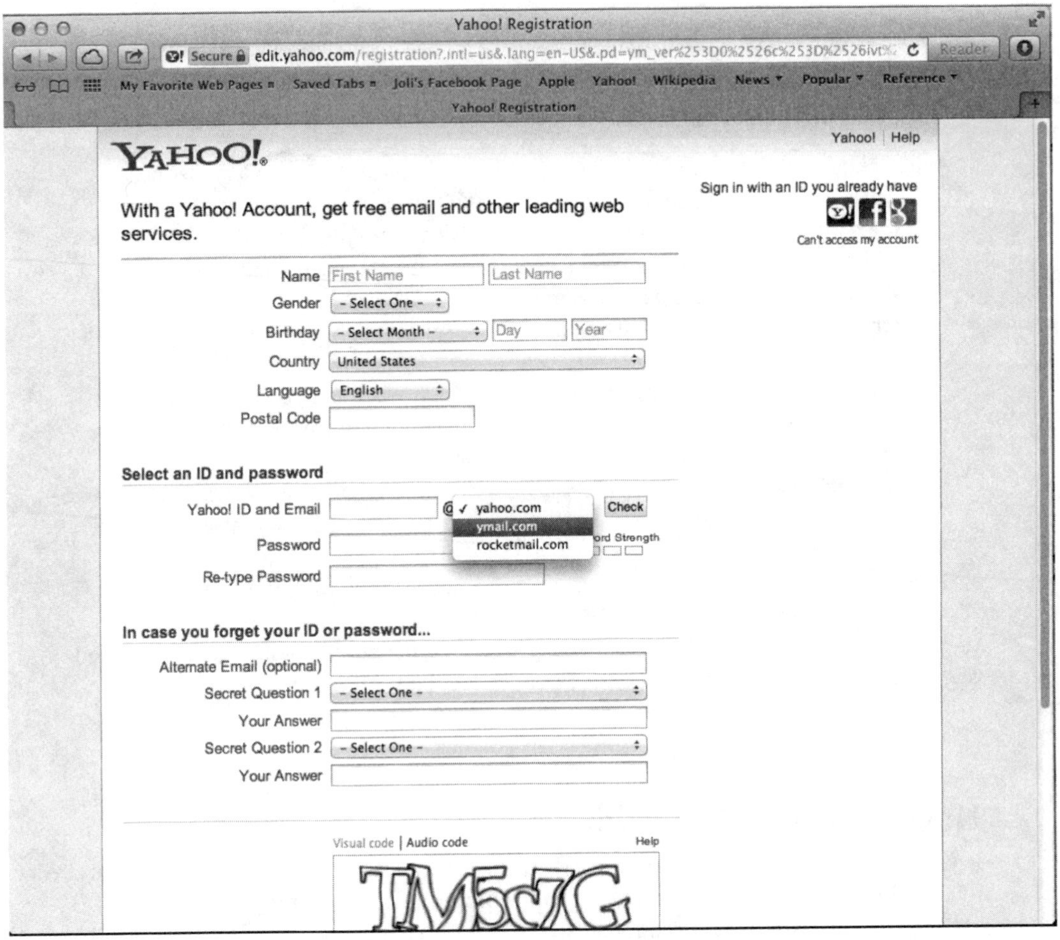

FIGURE 6-1   Yahoo! Mail has more domain extensions than @yahoo.com. You can choose an address with @ymail.com or @rocketmail.com.

If you have a Yahoo! Plus account (a paid account), you get up to 500 aliases you can use as disposable email addresses for shopping and using the Internet. If you have this type of account, go to Option and then select Mail Options to set up a disposable email address for use on the Web. With one of these addresses, you can opt to have any message from that account sent directly to a specific folder in your Yahoo! Mail to help you filter through your incoming mail. If the email address you use online is starting to fill up with unwanted messages, you can be sure that spammers got ahold of it, so you can dump the email address.

Configure Junk Email Preferences

You may notice that Mail highlights some of the mail in your Inbox as Junk and includes a message above the note saying, "Mail thinks this message is Junk."

For example, it automatically flags messages from senders who aren't in your address book or to whom you haven't recently sent a message. You can either flag the message as junk or not junk. Over time, Mail keeps all this information in a database and gets better at identifying what is junk and what isn't.

If you trust that Mail is sorting your junk mail appropriately, the following steps describe how you can change the preferences to send the mail consistently identified as "junk" to a Junk mailbox rather than having it show up in your Inbox.

Note   If you don't have the junk mail filter enabled and haven't yet used it, select the check box next to Enable junk mail filtering in the Junk Mail pane in Preferences. To make the filter work appropriately, spend some time determining what is junk and what isn't and then follow the steps here to move the junk to the Junk mailbox.

1. Click Mail in the menu and select Preferences or press COMMAND-comma.
2. Click the Junk Mail tab.
3. Under "When junk mail arrives," select the radio button next to Move it to the Junk mailbox.

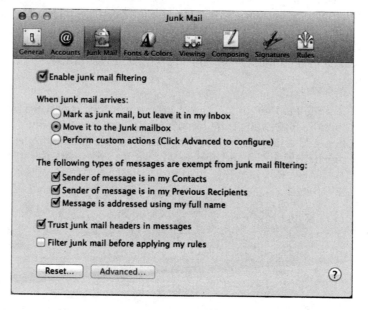

4. Confirm that you want to move junk mail by clicking the Move button when prompted. After this step you should see a new Junk mailbox beneath the mailboxes in the left column of Mail.
5. Check whether your Mail preferences are set to automatically delete mail in the Junk mailbox, by looking at the Mailbox Behaviors preferences pane. Go to the Mail menu and select Preferences or press COMMAND-comma.

6. Click the Accounts tab at the top of the window, and then select Mailbox Behaviors.
7. Select the email account you want to view if you have more than one.
8. Check the Delete Junk Message When pop-up menu is set to Never.
9. Check the other email accounts in Mail to apply the same setting, and then close the window.

If you think that Mail isn't sorting your junk properly and you still see a lot of unsolicited notes in your Inbox, you can reset the filter and start "teaching" Mail once again what is spam and what isn't. If you see a message that isn't flagged as junk, but should be, select the message in your inbox and click the icon that looks like a thumb pointing down. Over time, Mail will build a database of criteria for junk and get better at sorting it out for you.

Create Rules for Certain Junk Mail

Rules help Mail filter your incoming mail and do things like send certain emails to Junk or to another folder. If you are plagued by email from a certain spammer, you can have Mail send those messages automatically to the Junk mailbox or even directly to the Trash. Often, asking spammers to remove you from their list only confirms to them that your address is active. Once they know they have a real person to dump spam onto, they won't stop and may even sell your address to others.

The following steps describe how to create a rule for a specific email address. The rule can be to send messages from a certain address directly to the Trash or to send it to Junk.

1. Click the Mail menu and select Preferences or press COMMAND-comma.
2. Click the Rules tab at the top of the Preferences window.
3. Click Add Rule and enter a name for the rule (for example, annoying spammer, ex-girlfriend, or whatever else you want to name it). See Figure 6-2.

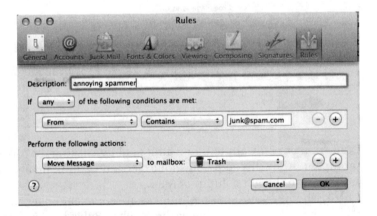

FIGURE 6-2 Set a rule to move messages from a certain email address directly to the Trash, Junk, or some other folder you choose.

4. Select From in the first pop-up menu and leave the second pop-up window with Contains showing.
5. Type the email address in the box after Contains.
6. Select a destination after Move Message to mailbox. You can choose Trash, Junk, or some other folder you created.

This isn't the most efficient way to manage spam, as new spammers pop up all the time and it's not viable to create a rule for every one of them. However, if you have one sender that you can't get rid of, this is one way to never have to see their messages again, especially if you send their notes directly to the Trash. Rules also come in handy for message types that you want to keep, like those from family members, certain friends, or even from a group you belong to. Setting up rules to manage these types of messages will be explored a little later in the chapter.

Clean Up Contacts

Contacts (or Address Book in OS X before Mountain Lion) is an application that keeps track of all the email addresses, telephone numbers, and other vital contact information of the people in your life. Contacts is available to multiple applications in OS X like Mail, Messages (formerly iChat), Calendar (formerly iCal), and the Address Book widget on your Dashboard. The information in Contacts can be synced to your iOS devices through iCloud, so you don't have to enter any of the information again on your device. Any updates you make to Contacts will be automatically pushed to your devices in Cloud (when you enable this option in iCloud and on your device). Over time, you'll probably find that you have duplicates of the same person or have an entry in Contacts that you don't use any more. Clean up this centralized tool so you have the most up-to-date information available to you when you are in Mail or when you are on the go with your iPhone or iPad.

Edit Contacts

In Mountain Lion you have a few options for viewing the cards in Contacts. You can opt to view one card at a time, a contact list and one contact, or a three-column view that includes (from left to right) a column with groups, the contact list, and a single contact. In each of these views you have an Edit button in the lower-left corner of the card. Click this button to edit the contact information for one of the cards in Contact.

The Edit function is especially handy if your contact's information doesn't fit with the existing card template. For example, this individual may have multiple email address, a Twitter account, or other information that you want to include but can't see where to enter it on the card other than in the Notes section. To add additional phone or fax details or custom information to a contact:

1. Launch Contacts by clicking the Dock icon.
2. Click the Contact card that you want to edit and click the Edit tab.

3. Click once on one of the double arrows next to the field name and select an option from the pop-up menu. You can add a pager number, or additional home or mobile number, among others. Enter the information for the new field.

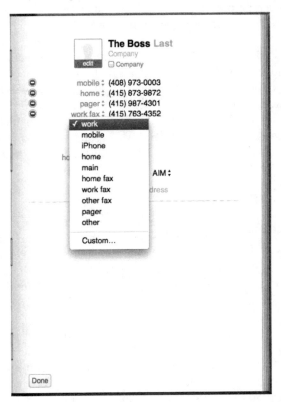

4. Select Custom from the pop-up menu if you want to add a field that isn't included in the contact card template. You can type in information like the contact's Facebook or Pinterest pages or a Twitter account.
5. Click the next set of double arrows to add additional fields and enter the information for those fields.
6. Click Done when you are finished entering new information for your contact.

Tip   You can add a photo of the person by double-clicking the Edit button in the picture field next to the contact name.

To change information in any of the fields on the card, click Edit, select the field information, and type over the existing entry. You can also completely delete a field by clicking the red minus (–) symbol next to the field.

To delete an entire card from Contacts, select the contact in List view and press DELETE, or click the Edit menu and select Delete Card. Confirm that you want to delete the card, and you're done.

To add a card, press COMMAND-N or click once on the plus (+) symbol at the bottom of the contact list column.

> **Tip** You can add email addresses to contact while you're in Mail. Select a message from the sender, click the Messages menu, and select Add Sender to Contacts.

Merge Duplicates

Having duplicates in contacts has a couple of common causes. You may have entered the data at different times and typed in slight variations to the person's name, or you may have two entries for one person because you entered their email address at one point and their phone number later on. You can get rid of duplicates and merge related contact information into one card.

Contacts offers an automated option for merging duplicates that merges the information without displaying it to you. The option outlined here is done manually, which can take a little longer, but affords you more control over the information being merged.

1. Flip through your contacts list and look for duplicate entries.
2. Select multiple, contiguous entries by pressing SHIFT-click or noncontiguous entries by pressing COMMAND-click.
3. Click Card from the menu and select Merge Selected Cards. You must have more than one card selected for the option to be enabled.

Once you merge the cards, if there is any conflicting information, the application selects one of the entries for the card and puts the conflicting information in the Notes field.

Create Groups with Contacts

If you regularly send messages to a group of people, you can save yourself time by creating a group. Rather than enter multiple email addresses, you enter one group address while composing an email, say a message to your extended family or maybe a club you belong to. To create a group in Contacts:

1. Click the File menu and select New Group.
2. Enter a name in the Group field in the far left column by typing over the default label "untitled group."
3. Click All Contacts to view the names and click and drag contacts into the group. You won't move the contact from your main list; you are creating a sort of alias when you drag them into the group folder.

> **Note** You can also create a group by selecting names from Contacts, clicking the File menu, and selecting New Group From Selection. A group name will appear in the first column, which you can type over and name whatever you like.

You can remove a contact from a group by doing the following:

1. Click the group in the first column.
2. Select a name in the group by clicking it once.
3. Go to the Edit menu and select Remove From Group.

Finally, you can delete the group while still preserving the contact information by selecting the group in the first column, clicking Edit, and selecting Delete Group.

Manage Mail

After you tidy Contacts and have sorted Spam, it's time to manage and organize the email you want to keep. If you belong to an online group, spend time on social media sites, or want to sort email from those close to you, you can filter those messages into specific folders to keep on top of the messages. There are other ways to view and manage your email as well, which will be explored in this section. Many of the functions overlap, and you can choose what will work for you to help you wade through your mail more efficiently to get to the good stuff right away.

Use the VIP Feature

You can promote a friend, family member, or colleague to VIP status, within Mail at least. This new feature for Mail in Mountain Lion allows you to identify a sender as a VIP and have their messages display in a special starred list.

You can more easily identify and view messages from these contacts. To designate someone as a VIP:

1. Select a message from a sender you want to (designate) as a VIP.
2. Hover your cursor on the left of the From field in the message until you see a grey star appear.

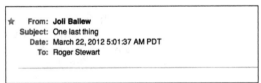

3. Click the star. Additional messages from the sender in your Inbox will appear with a star after you do this.
4. Once you have your designated VIPs, a VIP box will appear beneath your Mailboxes column, as shown here. When you click the sender's name, all messages from that person will display.

You can utilize the VIP feature in other ways as well, including creating rules for messages from VIPs, which will be explored shortly, or setting notifications to alert you when you receive an email from a VIP.

Create Mailboxes and Smart Mailboxes

A basic mailbox in Mail works like a folder where you can file any messages you may want to keep, like those from family, friends, or perhaps a special project at work. Your messages arrive in your mailbox normally and you file them into the Mailbox folder you made. A Smart Mailbox is one that effectively does the filing for you based on criteria (called *conditions*) that you set. Essentially, they work as an ongoing search for the conditions you create. Use Smart Mailboxes to keep on top of important messages in Mail and organize your incoming email.

To create a basic mailbox:

1. Click the Mailbox menu and select Create New Mailbox.
2. For Location, select On My Mac. This will create a folder beneath the On My Mac section of the sidebar in Mail.

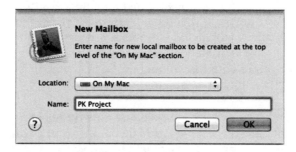

3. Click OK when you are done.

You can select the mail that you want to file by dragging into the new mailbox. Once you have a Mailbox folder set up, you can create and manage rules for those, which will be explored shortly. If you find you no longer need the folder or are at the end of a project, delete the mailbox by clicking the Mailbox window and selecting Delete Mailbox.

To create a Smart Mailbox, follow this example, which files all messages from family members in a separate mailbox.

1. Click the Mailbox menu and select New Smart Mailbox.
2. Enter a name for the Mailbox.
3. Click the first pop-up list and select one criteria. You can select based on who the message is from, the date received, a flagged message, a high-priority message, and more. The example in Figure 6-3 is based on who the mail is from.
4. Select an option from the second pop-up list. The options include Contains/ does not contain, Begins with/ends with, and Is equal to.
5. Add another criteria by clicking the plus (+) symbol next to the first criteria and repeat the process from Step 4.

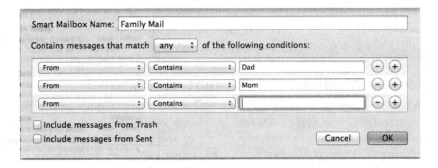

FIGURE 6-3 Create a Smart Mailbox based on criteria you set, such as who the message is from, when it was received, or a number of other options.

6. Select "any" from the pop-up menu near the top of the window if you created more than one criteria. If you choose "all," then Mail has to meet all of the criteria for the mailbox.
7. Select the check boxes next to Include Messages from Trash and Include Messages from Sent. If you inadvertently delete an important message, your Smart Mailbox will include it in its search. If you replied to an important message (one that meets the criteria set for your Mailbox), you can keep your reply together with the original message.
8. Click OK when you are done.

You can edit the Smart Mailbox at any time by selecting it, clicking Mailbox from the menu, and selecting Edit Smart Mailbox. When you want to delete the mailbox, click the Mailbox menu and select Delete Mailbox.

Create and Manage Rules for Mail

Rules help you filter incoming messages by doing things like moving unsolicited email into Junk, alerting you to important messages, and filing messages directly into your mailboxes for you. As with Smart Mailboxes, you select the criteria, called conditions, to help Mail perform the functions you want it to. The process of creating rules is similar to the steps for creating a Smart Mailbox, but rules can perform actions with your messages. Here is a short list of some of the actions you can choose from:

- Move selected messages to a basic Mailbox folder, Trash, Junk, or Archive.
- Copy selected messages to a basic Mailbox folder, Trash, Junk, or Archive.
- Play a sound when a message is received.
- Reply, forward, or redirect a message.
- Delete a message.

You can create a rule to file all the dozens (hundreds?) of emails from social media sites directly to a mailbox folder, set a sound notification when you receive an email from your boss, or create rules for email from coworkers that you are collaborating with on a particular project. There are many more possibilities as well. To get started creating rules for Mail, do the following:

1. Go to the Mail menu and select Preferences or press COMMAND-comma.
2. Click the Rules tab at the top of the window.
3. Click Add Rule and name the rule you want to create in the Description field.
4. Click the first pop-up menu and select from one of the options. You can choose a condition based on who the message is from, what the subject is, and the date received or sent, among others (see Figure 6-4).
5. Select another condition in the next pop-up menu. Some examples are Contains/does not contain, Begins with/ends with, and Is equal to.
6. Click the plus (+) symbol if you want to add an additional rule.
7. Select the "any" option at the top when you make more than one rule so that the rule will apply if any one of the conditions is met.
8. Choose an action for Mail to perform when the conditions in your rule are met. For example, you may want the messages moved or copied to a different folder, highlighted with a color, or replied to automatically.
9. Click the (+) symbol and select Stop Evaluating Rules from the pop-up menu. This ensures that another rule doesn't move the message after the first rule has been applied.
10. Click OK when you finish selecting the conditions for your rule.

FIGURE 6-4 Create a rule to send messages from selected contacts directly to a mailbox of your choice.

Remove Attachments from Messages

Once you have downloaded an email attachment, you can delete it from the message (while keeping the message) to save on disk space. You can delete attachments from the Sent folder as well to keep from gunking up Mail. Once you download (or send) an attachment, select the message, click Message from the menu, and select Remove Attachments. The email message will be preserved and the attachment will no longer be clogging up your mailbox.

Watch the Size of Your Sent and Deleted Folders

If you have more than one email account linked to Mail, you may have hundreds or even thousands of messages in your Sent and Deleted folders. Keep an eye on these and try to keep only the messages you really think you'll need. Some people are uncommonly attached to their email messages. You can configure a few preferences for Trash to help you with the housekeeping. The Mail application has its own Trash and is set by default to empty deleted messages after a month. To choose to empty your Trash sooner, do the following:

1. Open Mail Preferences by pressing COMMAND-comma.
2. Click the Accounts tab.
3. Choose an account.
4. Click the Mailbox Behaviors tab.
5. Select a different option (One Day Old/One Week Old).

7

Optimize Safari
and Stay Safe Online

Of all the applications that come with Mac OS X, Safari is one of the most popular and the one most people know something about. Whether you use it only occasionally or have it open continually on its own desktop, there are several things you can do to optimize Safari to make it suit the way you work. In this chapter we explore some of the things you can do to personalize your browser, including managing how you view sites and collect and file your favorite bookmarks. The second half of the chapter will look at how to keep your personal information safe while browsing by managing cookies and using the Private Browsing option.

Personalize Safari

Safari in Mountain Lion comes with some new features that can help you streamline and improve your browsing experience. Some of the older features are still available, including almost all of the features added with Lion. You can customize many of the features to help you work more efficiently and keep yourself organized while you surf.

 If you were a fan of the RSS feed option in Safari, you may be disappointed to learn that this feature is no longer in Mountain Lion. The RSS feed displayed synopses of articles from news or blogs on the right of your Safari screen. If one caught your attention, you simply clicked the link and went straight to the article on your favorite site.

Choose a Search Engine and Your Home Page

In Mountain Lion, the search function and the address bar have merged into one long field at the top of your browser, as shown in Figure 7-1. You can type a URL into the address bar to get straight to a web site, or you can type in a keyword to perform a simple web search. The address bar also has a predictive text option; type in the first few letters of a URL, and several suggestions display beneath the address bar. If you have a preference for one search engine over another, you can set Safari to search with your preferred search engine.

FIGURE 7-1 New address bar in Mountain Lion with the address field and search function in one place

When you first open your browser, you are taken to Apple's home page. You can choose another page to display when you launch Safari, whether a favorite sports site, news site, or maybe your favorite social network home page. To configure your preferred search engine and home page:

1. Press COMMAND-comma or click the Safari menu and select Preferences.
2. In the General pane, select a default search engine from the pop-up menu (Google, Yahoo!, or Bing).

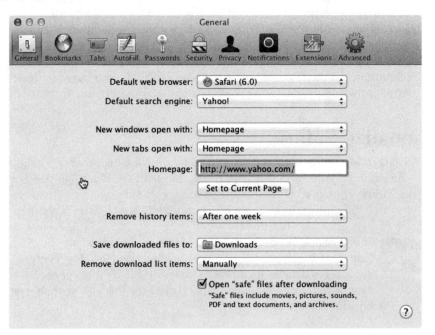

3. Go to the page you want to use as your home, and then click the Set to Current Page button. If the URL for your page doesn't display in Preferences, you can copy and paste the URL.
4. Close Preferences when you are done.

Note A new feature in Mountain Lion lets you share a web page with just one click. Look for the share icon (it looks like an arrow coming out of a box) and click it while you're on a site to share it directly via an email message, through Messages or on Twitter.

Add a Web Site to the Bookmarks Bar

If you frequently visit one news site or are a social media addict or have a web site you visit more than any other, you can add those sites to the Bookmarks Bar at the top of Safari to get to those web sites with just one click. Bookmarks residing in the Bookmarks Bar differ from other bookmarks because they always display in the Bookmarks Bar, so you don't have to navigate to a folder to access the site. These types of bookmarks display as buttons with a text label, and a few of these will be included by default, including Apple, Yahoo!, and Google Maps. To add a site directly to the Bookmarks Bar for quick, one-click access, do any of the following:

- Drag the site's icon (the tiny image that displays on the far left of the URL) directly into the Bookmarks Bar. A green plus (+) sign will appear and when you release the URL, it will display in your Bookmarks Bar.
- Visit the site and click the Bookmarks Menu and Select Add Bookmark. Select Bookmarks Bar from the pop-up menu.
- Press COMMAND-D while on the site, then add to the Bookmarks Bar.

You can rearrange the bookmarks by clicking and dragging them sideways within the bar. The position of the other bookmarks will adjust automatically. To remove a site from your Bookmarks Bar, click and drag it out of the Bookmarks Bar. It will disappear in a puff of smoke.

Manage Bookmarks Folders

When you added bookmarks to Safari, you saved them either to one of the folders in the Bookmarks Bar or in the Bookmarks Menu. The best way to organize your bookmarks is to use the folders in the Bookmarks Bar or create your own folders in the Bookmarks Bar (see Figure 7-2). The small arrow icons next to Popular and My Favorite Web Pages in your Bookmarks Bar are examples of these types of folders. You access bookmarks by clicking the folder and selecting the web site you want to view. You can create new folders here or edit and delete existing folders.

To view your bookmarks, navigate to your Bookmarks library. With Safari open, do the following:

1. Click the Bookmarks Menu icon (it looks like a little book).
2. Click the Bookmarks Bar icon in the left column of the screen, beneath History. All the items in your Bookmarks Bar, including the folders, will display at the bottom of the page.
3. Click the arrow next to a folder to view its contents.

You can delete a web site from the folder by selecting it and pressing DELETE, or rearrange the order of the bookmarks by dragging them up and down the list. If you don't want a folder to display in the Bookmarks Bar, select it and press DELETE. You can also move a web site from one folder into another. Open both folders and click and drag on the web site, and then release it in the folder you want to file it in.

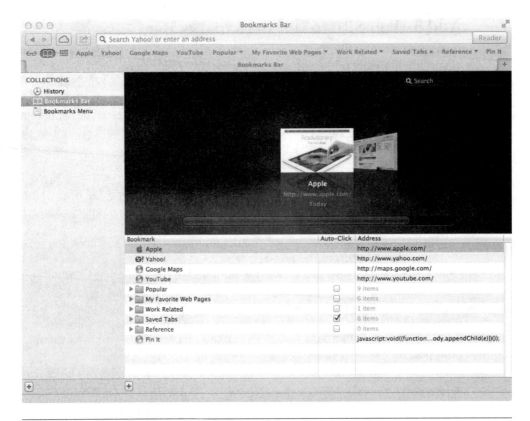

FIGURE 7-2 The web sites and folders in the Bookmarks Bar in Safari

You can add new folders by clicking the plus symbol immediately beneath the list of sites in the Bookmarks Bar. A new folder will display and you can type over the label and enter a name of your choice.

As you browse, you can add sites to the folder by pressing COMMAND-D and then selecting the folder name from the pop-up list that displays. The next time you want to access the site, you simply click the arrow next to the folder name in your Bookmarks Bar and select the site from the pop-up list.

 With iCloud, you can add a bookmark on your computer or device, and it can be added to the bookmarks on your other devices or computers. You have to enable this option in your iCloud preferences and on your device in Settings.

View Web Pages More Effectively

Safari comes with a number of built-in features to help you make the most of your surfing sessions. Some of these features, like tabbed browsing and the Bookmarks Bar, will help you organize your favorite stuff from the Internet. These features and more will be explored in this section.

Use Full-Screen Mode and Gestures in Safari

You can navigate your way around the Internet much as you do on an iPad, iPhone, or iPod touch when you activate full-screen mode in Safari. To activate full-screen mode, click the double arrows in the upper-right corner of your browser, and Safari will take up every available pixel of your screen. If you have a small monitor, this is a great way to get the most out of your favorite web sites. The best way to navigate through web pages in this mode is through Multi-Touch gestures, including:

- Use a two-fingered swipe across the trackpad. Swipe left to go back a page and right to move forward one page.
- Pinch and expand two fingers on the trackpad to zoom in or out.
- Double-tap on the trackpad on a selected block of text or graphics to magnify only that selection.

You can also navigate through Safari without a mouse by using the TAB key to move to the next field or pop-up menu. You can hold down the OPTION-TAB key to jump through the links and buttons on the page. When you press the RETURN key, the highlighted link will open.

 If you have more than one full-screen app open at the same time, each will have its own desktop in Mission Control. To switch between screens, swipe sideways on your trackpad with three fingers to navigate back and forth. Other apps like Mail, Calendar, and iPhoto have the full-screen option.

Configure and Use Tabbed Browsing

Rather than have multiple windows open for each web page, you can keep all of your sites in one window with tabbed browsing, which is enabled by default in Mountain Lion. To jump back and forth to sites, you simply click one of the tabs at the top of the browser. If you are using Lion, Snow Leopard, or Leopard, you can enable tabbed browsing in Safari Preferences under Tabs. Select Automatically from the pop-up menu next to Open pages in tabs instead of windows.

Tabbed browsing comes in especially handy when you have a set of web sites that you frequent each day. You can add all of these sites into one folder in the Bookmarks Bar that is labeled Saved Tabs. If you include the web sites with the Bookmarks Bar option, you click once and have a set of your favorite pages open, organized by tabs, all in one window, as shown here.

To add a web site to your Saved Tabs:

1. Navigate to one of your favorite web sites so it displays in Safari.
2. Click and drag the site's URL or site icon to the Saved Tabs folder in your Bookmarks Bar. The Saved Tabs should be highlighted and you will see a green plus (+) symbol. Release the URL into the folder.
3. Type a name for the site when prompted to name the bookmark and click OK.

You can view any of the folders in your Bookmarks Bar in tabbed browsing. Click the folder name (Popular, My Favorite Web Pages, and so on) and select Open in Tabs. All the sites in the folder will open in one window.

Finally, occasionally when you're surfing, you won't want to use tabbed browsing. Perhaps you want to view two sites in side-by-side windows, for example. To open a page in a window instead of a tab, press COMMAND-OPTION and then click the link. You can also change Safari Preferences to open pages in windows. To do this, go into Safari Preferences by pressing COMMAND-comma. Click Tabs in the top of the window and select Never from the pop-up menu at the top.

Use Reading List

Rather than bookmark an entire web site, you can keep track of pages you want to read later or save a video to watch when you have free time. Using Reading List is simpler than configuring bookmarks, and you can navigate back and forth to your reading list with just one click. The list is saved in a column that you can show or hide to the left of your browser by clicking the glasses icon in the top left of Safari. You can add a page to Reading List by doing any of the following:

- Press SHIFT-COMMAND-D.
- When Reading List is open, click the Add Page button to have the current page added to your list.
- Click Bookmarks in the menu and select Add to Reading List.

When you have the Reading List column open in Safari, you can sort the pages by clicking the All or Unread buttons at the top of the column, as shown here.

To delete a page when you are done reading it, point your cursor to the right side of the item in the list and when an X appears, click it once to delete. You can also delete all the items in your list by clicking the Clear All button at the top. When you are finished using Reading List, click the glasses icon to close it.

Use Safari Reader

You can more easily read an article or blog when you use Reader in Safari. When available, Reader eliminates everything in the page except the text and images. There are no annoying ads, banners, or links—just a clean white background with easy-to-read text and a few images, as shown in the following illustration. The main web site will dim in the background while you read the article in plain text. Reader isn't available to use with every web page and only works with an article rather than an entire web page. You'll know if Reader is accessible when the large Reader button at the top of Safari on the right changes color from grey to blue.

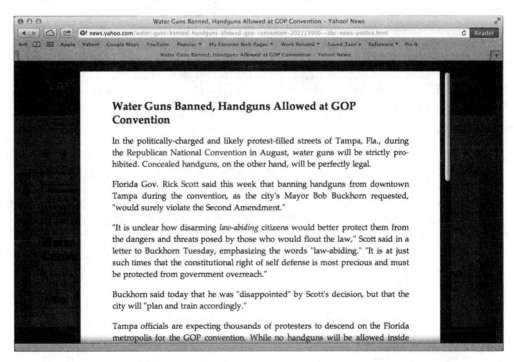

To get the most out of Reader, make sure that you are in an article page rather than the main web site page. There are some instances when Reader won't work, including when sites use Flash or other options for displaying page content. When it is available, it is a truly great way to read content in Safari.

To exit Reader, simply click once on the Reader button at the top of Safari.

Secure Safari: The Basics

We all spend a good deal of time on the Internet each day reading the news, shopping, and checking in to social sites, but we put ourselves at some risk each time we do so. At each site you visit (even the ones you click accidentally), you can leave a little bit of your personal information. Here are some of the ways you leave information about yourself while using Safari—or any browser—while using the Internet:

- **Visiting a web site**   The server on the web site may record the time of your visit, the pages you viewed, your IP address, or the type of web browser you use.
- **Entering data into a form**   If you are on an unencrypted site (one without the https: preceding the URL), then potentially anyone can view the information you submit. This information can be stored or passed along to others (spammers, and so on).
- **Browsing with Safari**   All the sites you visit are recorded in Safari's history. This makes it easy for you to revisit sites you forgot to bookmark, and also helps Safari configure your Top Sites. However, if you share a user account with someone else, you may not want that person to be privy to all the sites you've visited.
- **Using Auto Fill to enter your user name and passwords**   Anyone who accesses your user account can log in with your information and can potentially use it to log in as you on forums or possibly view your financial or personal information on the sites you frequent.

There are several things you can do to prevent the unintended transmission of your information over the Internet. One of the most important and simplest ways to protect yourself is to use secure sites wherever possible. A secure site should have an https: and a padlock symbol in the URL. If you enter information into a secure form, it can't be viewed by a third party. If the site has a secure option, you should be automatically directed to the secure site. For example, Facebook now has a secure option, which will redirect you to the encrypted site, even if you type www.facebook.com in your address bar. There are more things you can do as well, ranging from managing the privacy settings in Safari to using Private Browsing to eliminate some of the risks described earlier.

Understand and Manage Cookies

When you first visit a web site by entering an address into your browser, a message is sent to the server of that web page asking for the page information. The web site sends the information to your browser but may also create a text file, called a *cookie*, that is stored on your computer. The web site will also keep a copy of that file. Cookies are created to enable a web site to remember information about you, and for the most part, they can be very useful.

There are different types of cookies, not all of them malicious. For example, if you frequent a shopping site, allowing cookies for that site will make it easier when you return to the site. Maybe you added items to the shopping cart but didn't check out—the next time you visit, your items are there in the shopping cart. If you searched for something on the site, on Amazon for example, your search is remembered and the items you previously viewed will be displayed in a sidebar on the site or otherwise highlighted for you so that you know what you looked at the last time you were on the site.

Cookies can create problems when a company or organization you didn't intend to have access to your cookies gets a hold of them. Some site owners share this information with their partners so that they can find out about your browsing and shopping habits and potentially target you with advertisements. These are referred to as third-party cookies. By default, Safari blocks third-party cookies. Say you visit a garden supply site looking for terra cotta pots. If third-party cookies aren't blocked, a separate web site can access this information and use it to create targeted advertising in your browser. For example, you may get ads from a different web site for terra cotta pots or some other gardening item popping up while you surf.

Finally, web sites can use cookies as a way to track the sites you visit while you surf. Tracking cookies keep a detailed account of where you have been on the Internet and can reveal a great deal of information about you. Tracking cookies are used by organizations or companies interested in either marketing to you themselves or selling information about your surfing habits to another organization so they can target you with their marketing offers.

To manage your privacy settings in Safari:

1. Select Preferences from the Safari menu or press COMMAND-comma.
2. Click the Privacy tab at the top of the window (see Figure 7-3). Confirm that third-party advertiser cookies are blocked. This should be selected by default, but if you changed it for some reason, consider changing it back. Select the radio button next to From third parties and advertisers to block these cookies.
3. Check that the option Limit web site access to location services is set to Deny without prompting, or choose another option if you prefer. If you deny a web site's access to location services, the servers for those web sites won't be able to tell where you are geographically. The "deny" option is selected by default in Mountain Lion.
4. Select the check box next to Ask web sites not to track me. Enabling this option may help prevent tracking cookies. It sends a message to the web site server asking it not to track you. However, the server doesn't have to comply with this request. At present, asking a web site not to track you is a matter of respect; some web sites may respect your request while others will ignore it.

Note If you do choose to enable location services in Safari, you will also have to change your Security and Privacy preferences in System Preferences. In the Privacy section, click the lock to make the changes, and then select the check box next to Enable Location Services. You may wish to enable this option to receive targeted advertising or to use with a social network.

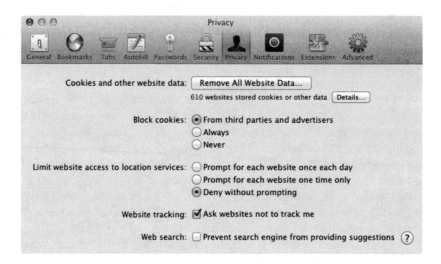

FIGURE 7-3   Configure how you want to block cookies in the Privacy pane of Safari Preferences.

Delete Selected Cookies

If your Mac contains cookies for sites you don't use or don't want to save cookies for, you can delete those cookies manually from your Mac. To delete cookies from your computer:

1. Select Preferences from the Safari menu or press COMMAND-comma.
2. Click the Privacy Preferences pane.
3. Click the Details button under the Remove All Website Data button. (If you click the Remove All Website Data button, every cookie from all the sites you've visited will be deleted.)
4. A new window will appear with a list of web sites that have stored data (see Figure 7-4). Web site cookies are included in this list, but so are other types of data like cache files and plug-ins.
5. Select the files that you want to delete by clicking once on the web site name. To delete only cookie files, select the sites that have stored cookies.
6. Click Remove to eliminate the file from your Mac, and then click Done when you are finished going through the list and deleting the cookies you want.

Caution   Deleting cookies from some web sites may make it difficult to access the content from the web site the next time you visit, or cause other problems. Only delete cookies for sites you are certain not to visit again.

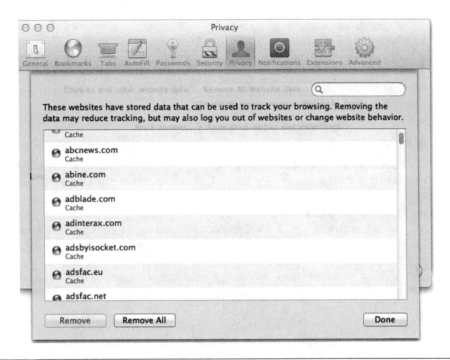

FIGURE 7-4   Cookies and other data residing on your Mac, which you can delete

Use Private Browsing

If you want to browse to your heart's content through any web page, without leaving a trail of information, you can use Private Browsing. When you opt to browse privately, the following happens with your browsing session:

- Sites are not added to Safari's history. This prevents other users of your user account from viewing the sites you visit. Temporary data is collected so that you can click back and forth between pages.
- Cookies you generate by visiting sites will be automatically deleted when you exit Safari.
- Cache, which is a type of file that is stored on your Mac and contains information about the web sites you visit, is deleted after you close Safari. Cache will be explored more in the next section.
- Search terms, which are ordinarily stored in Safari, aren't kept in the recent searches list.
- Anything you download won't display in the Downloads list, but you will still need to delete it manually if you want to remove it from your Mac.
- Safari doesn't retain any information you enter into web forms like credit card details, user names, and passwords.

To use this option, simply click the Safari menu and select Private Browsing. A check mark will display next to Private Browsing in the menu and your address bar will display PRIVATE in the upper-right corner. When you are done with your Private Browsing session, deselect Private Browsing from the menu and be sure to close any window you opened while in that mode. When you open Safari again, it will open in normal browsing mode.

Empty the Cache

Cache files store information that you use to browse web pages. When you first visit a web site, Safari stores images and other content from the site in cache files so the next time you visit the site, it loads more quickly. Cache files are there to enhance the performance of Safari and make it easier for you to visit your favorite sites.

Occasionally, cache files can become corrupted or cause problems while you browse. Safari may slow down, take forever to open, or even crash while you are surfing. You can try deleting cache files as a troubleshooting step if you are having any of these problems and see whether doing so restores performance or stops problems you're having. To delete the Safari cache, do the following:

1. Open Safari Preferences by pressing COMMAND-comma.
2. Click the Advanced button and select the check box next to Show Develop menu in menu bar. You should see Develop appear in the menu after you select this.
3. Click the Develop menu in Safari and select Empty Cache.

There is a lot of advice out there about cache files. Much of the advice about cache encourages you to delete cache regularly or portrays cache files as problematic in their own right. They're actually there to help, and you should only consider emptying cache if you've noticed problems with Safari like slowing down or some other quirks. Deleting some cache files may help resolve some of these problems if you can find no other cause.

Reset Safari

If you haven't used the Private Browsing option and want to prevent other users of your Mac from seeing the web sites you've visited, using your saved user names and passwords, and otherwise preserving some of your privacy, you have a reset option you can employ. To reset Safari, go to the Safari menu and select Reset Safari. You can clear the check boxes next to items you don't want to reset.

Some of the items that you can reset in the reset menu are as follows:

- **Clear history**   Clears the list of sites you have been on.
- **Reset Top Sites**   Undoes any changes you've made to Top Sites.
- **Remove all web page preview images**   Clears the thumbnail images Safari saves of the pages you view.
- **Reset all location warnings**   Clears information about your location that web sites have collected about you.
- **Remove all web site data**   Web site data includes things like cookies, cache, and other file types related to the sites you've visited.
- **Remove saved names and passwords**   Deletes the user names and passwords that Safari fills in automatically in web forms (if you enabled AutoFill).
- **Clear the Downloads list**   The list in Downloads will be cleared, but the actual downloaded files themselves may reside elsewhere on your computer.
- **Close all Safari windows**   Prevents others from using the Back and Forward buttons to view the web sites you've been on.

Once you have finished clearing the check boxes for the items you don't want to include in the reset, click the Reset button at the bottom.

Install Safari Extensions to Block Tracking Cookies and Ads

Extensions are features that you can add to Safari to improve or augment your web browsing. You can add extensions to monitor activity on your favorite social sites, keep track of what you are selling on eBay, or improve online video viewing. There are also many just-for-fun extensions that update you when new game releases for your favorite gaming platform are available. Extensions display as little icons in your toolbar that you can interact with. Extensions can come in especially handy when you want to block annoying ads from displaying and also prevent networks and companies from tracking your web activity. These types of extensions are explored next.

To get extensions, go to the Safari menu and select Safari Extensions. You are taken to Apple's secure Safari Extensions Gallery web site. You can browse through the popular section or go straight to the Security menu on the left side of the screen and click Security.

Do Not Track Plus (DNT+) is an extension that alerts you when a web site you visit tries to track activity and potentially share it with partners or other advertisers. DNT+ operates by blocking "requests" from servers, usually those belonging to tracking companies or advertisers but also social media sites. When these tracking requests are denied by DNT+, any company trying to track you will be blocked from tracking you by putting tracking cookies on your server. The company that created this extension keeps a growing list of known tracking companies and organizations as well as social networks. Blocking prevents advertiser or other data collecting companies from gathering or sharing your data.

To install DNT+, locate it in the Security extensions on Apple's site and click Install Now. The extension is installed in Safari in one click. Once installed, it will display in Safari's toolbar as an icon to the left of your address bar.

DNT+ can stop third-party sites from putting cookies on your Mac and seeing the web sites you've visited. It can provide you with some control over whether your web activities are tracked. The program can also help you send an "opt out" message to advertisers to request that they not target you with ads.

To use DNT+, follow these steps:

1. Enter the address of a web site you frequent or select a site from your bookmarks.
2. A small red alert bubble will display over the Do Not Track Plus icon in your toolbar if the web site you are on is sharing your data.
3. Click the alert bubble to display the list of other companies and networks tracking you (see Figure 7-5). You may see social network sites like Facebook and Twitter, ad networks, or other companies in the lists.
4. Click the ad networks section, if displayed. In this section you can send a message to ad networks to opt out of their targeted advertising. To do this, click the Click to Opt out Of Advertising link. You will be taken to the Abine company web site, the makers of DNT+. On this page, click the Opt Me Out Now button.

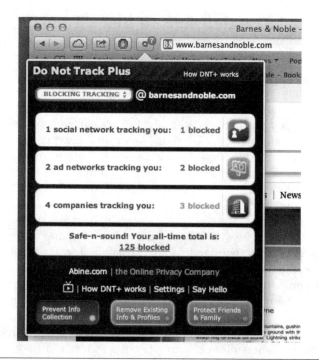

FIGURE 7-5   Number of organizations or companies tracking your activity on the current page

5. Click the "companies tracking you" section of the DNT+ pop-up screen. A list of companies tracking you will display as well as the action taken by DNT+ (see Figure 7-6). In some cases, DNT+ suggests that you don't block certain sites. It usually does this to preserve the functionality of the site. Blocking some sites may prevent features of the site from working properly. You can override the suggestion by clicking once on the site in the list to block tracking.
6. Monitor the DNT+ icon in your toolbar and repeat Steps 1-5 as you browse and visit new web sites.

FIGURE 7-6   A detailed list of the networks and companies DNT+ blocked from accessing your visit information

The Opt Out function, if selected, creates new cookies on your Mac. These cookies are used to tell web sites not to track you. If you delete cookies in the Privacy pane of Safari Preferences, you will need to repeat the "opt out" process with DNT+.

There are other security extensions for Safari that you can explore as well, including AdBlock, and extensions that target specific social networks. Most social networks encourage you to "share" your web activities, but this is also one way that they keep track of where you go and what you are interested in. You can add extensions with one click on the Apple extensions page, but to manage them you need to work within Safari Preferences. To uninstall or alter an extension, click COMMAND-comma or go to the Safari menu and select Preferences. Click the Extensions pane to uninstall an extension, update it, or manage options (if offered).

8   Take Control of Mountain Lion

In the summer of 2011, Apple took a step in the direction of turning your Mac into a rather large iPad. The release of OS X 10.7, known as Lion, brought with it many features of iPad and other iOS devices including full-screen apps, AutoSave options, and Launchpad—which is a dead ringer for your iOS home screen. With Mountain Lion, the push toward an iOS-like interface went a little bit further with the inclusion of features like Notifications, Messages, Notes, Share Sheets, and more developed iCloud functions. While the changes brought by these new releases of OS X are exciting and useful for the most part, some things can be a little confusing, and others are downright frustrating. This chapter will highlight some of the features in Mountain Lion that you'll want to understand and work with, like iCloud, AutoSave, and Versions. We'll also give you a few tips on how to configure your new operating system to work the way you want it to—in some cases by changing or disabling the features you may not like.

Mountain Lion is used for examples throughout this chapter. You can work with many of the same features in Lion if you haven't yet upgraded to Mountain Lion. Throughout this chapter, we've noted where the features are not available in Lion.

Understand What Mountain Lion Has to Offer

If you use an iPhone, iPod, or iPad, some of the features in Mountain Lion will be very familiar to you. Many of the apps that have been added to your Mac are fun and useful, like Game Center, Notifications, and Notes. However, in terms of keeping your Mac healthy, the syncing and backup options offered in iCloud in Mountain Lion are exceptionally helpful. If you work on more than one Mac, or a Mac and one or more iOS devices, iCloud makes it possible to sync the data from many of your apps across all your devices and computers with minimal effort on your part. You don't have to re-enter and manage your data and documents with a complex file system or transfer them across devices manually. In fact, with many apps you don't even have to remember to save your work. In this next section we take a look at how iCloud works and how you can use it to manage data on multiple devices or computers.

Make Use of iCloud

iCloud is Apple's cloud computing service that stores and backs up your data from your apps on a central server. Once enabled, iCloud pushes your data wirelessly to all the devices and computers set up with your iCloud account so that content you add to your computer will also sync to your device. For example, if you add a telephone or email address to Contacts, those details will show up on your iPhone automatically. If you are in the middle of a chat on Messages, you can start on your Mac and then continue it on the go with your iPhone. The iCloud service also performs backups of your data once a day, like the content you purchase from the App Store, your device settings, photos, and more. While it doesn't actually store your iTunes purchases, it keeps track of what you've purchased so that if you need to restore your device from backup, your purchases will automatically download again. The information is stored in an encrypted format to protect your privacy.

Note   To use iCloud for syncing and backing up your device data and iTunes purchases, you need to have iTunes 10.5, and you need to have iOS 5 running on your device. Devices that support iOS 5 include the iPhone 3GS, iPhone 4, iPhone 4S, 3rd and 4th generation iPod touch, and all iPad devices.

You also have the option to save some of your documents to your iCloud account in Mountain Lion. You get 5GB of free space to store your data as well as any iCloud-enabled apps like those in the iWork suite or TextEdit. The content you purchase in iTunes doesn't count against your storage, so the 5GB can be utilized for mail, documents, and other app data. If you do run out of room, you can buy more storage from 15GB for $20 a year to 55GB for $100 annually. The really handy thing about iCloud is that it syncs all of your information across your computer and any Apple devices you own that are registered with your Apple ID.

If you didn't sign in to iCloud when you first upgraded to Mountain Lion, you can do so through your System Preferences. Open System Preferences and click the iCloud icon to get to the screen shown here. Enter your Apple ID and password, and then click Sign In.

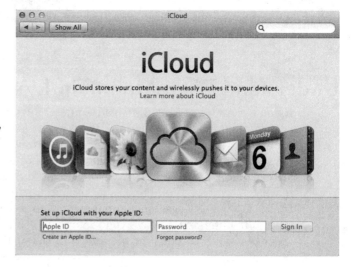

Once you sign in to iCloud, you will be taken through a series of setup screens to enable iCloud to sync content in your apps, and to do things like set up your free @me.com iCloud email account. The options that you can select are discussed next. When you log in to iCloud, the first screen you see will ask you whether you want to include Contacts, Calendars, and Bookmarks and also the Find My Mac option. If you opt for Find My Mac, location services have to be enabled on your Mac. You can change this setting if it's not active by going to System Preferences and clicking Security & Privacy. To allow your apps to determine your location, select the check box next to Enable Location Services. To configure the other items you want to use in iCloud, select or clear the check boxes next to the application you want to use with iCloud, as shown in Figure 8-1.

- **Mail**   You get a free me.com email account with iCloud, which you can access through your Mac, your devices, or through your browser via icloud.com.
- **Contacts**   The data in your Contacts, like phone numbers, mailing addresses, businesses' information, or fax numbers, are synced across devices when you select this check box. If you enter data on one device, it will be automatically pushed to all your devices.
- **Calendars & Reminders**   All your daily activities, appointments, meetings, and reminders you set for yourself will be pushed to any device or computer registered with your Apple ID. You also have the option to share your calendar with other iCloud users. (You won't have the Reminders option if you haven't upgraded to Mountain Lion.)

FIGURE 8-1   iCloud options to choose from when you log in to your iCloud account for the first time or when you open System Preferences and iCloud

- **Bookmarks**   iCloud keeps tracks of web pages you bookmark and syncs them with your other computers and devices so that if you bookmark a page on your Mac, you can access them while you are out and about with your iPhone or iPod touch.
- **Notes**   The Notes feature, which is new in Mountain Lion, will automatically push any entries you add to Notes to your devices and computers registered with your Apple ID.
- **Photo Stream**   When you enable this option, the photos you take on any iOS device or download to your Mac from your digital camera will sync over Wi-Fi to your devices, and to iPhoto or Aperture on your Mac. iCloud keeps 1000 of your most recent photos in the Photo Stream album.
- **Documents & Data**   The data you enter and edit in any iWork apps will be backed up to iCloud. If you don't own the iWork app, you can make use of iCloud storage with TextEdit and Preview in Mountain Lion. The documents you edit and create in TextEdit and Preview are saved automatically and set to save to iCloud by default.
- **Back to My Mac**   This option allows you to connect to your Mac remotely over the Internet and control the keyboard and cursor and access any files on your Macintosh HD. If you need files from your Mac while you are away from it, you can email them to yourself at the computer you are using to access your Mac remotely. If you select this option in iCloud Preferences, you need to set up your router to get the most out of Back to My Mac. Once you select the check box, you are prompted to do this.
- **Find My Mac**   Locates your Mac or device on a map if you misplace it. Once your device or computer is located, you can lock it remotely, have it play an alert message, or reset it to factory settings so that anyone who finds it will be unable to access your personal data.

After you select what you want to use with iCloud, you can go back into System Preferences at any time to manage your iCloud account. If you clear one of the check boxes, you will get a window asking if you want to keep or delete the data associated with the app you are disabling from iCloud.

Enable iCloud Settings on Your Devices

If you don't want all your data pushed to your devices, you can limit what you want synced and still make use of iCloud storage features. Your devices must be running iOS 5 or later for this to work. Turn on iCloud on your device by doing the following:

1. Tap Settings and tap the iCloud icon.
2. Enter your Apple ID and password.
3. Tap On to enable any of the features on your device. All the settings you have on your Mac iCloud window will appear here, including Mail, Contacts, Calendars, Reminders, Bookmarks, Notes, Photo Stream, Documents & Data, and Find My iPhone (or iPad). For example, if you don't want Notes or Photo Stream to sync on your iPhone, check that those are turned off.
4. At the bottom of the iCloud window, tap Storage & Backup to enable iCloud to store and back up your data. Turn the iCloud Backup icon on. You can also buy more storage here.

View Your iCloud Account and Try the Find My ... Function

Log in to your iCloud account from Safari or any other browser at icloud.com. All you need to log in to your account is your Apple ID and password. From here, you can get an overview of the content in your iCloud account and log in to your me.com mail account. If you have the iWork suite of apps, or even just one iWork app like Pages, you can view and edit your current documents here. Your Contacts are also accessible. You can view and edit contact information and it will sync automatically across your computers and devices. Finally, you can keep tabs on a lost device (or one that slipped behind your sofa) by utilizing the Find My iPhone feature, as shown in Figure 8-2.

1. Log in to iCloud with your ID and password.
2. Click the Find My iPhone icon.
3. Once your device is located on the map, click the blue Info icon. You have three options to choose from: click Play Sound or Send Message (which will help you locate your device if it's nearby); click Remote Lock to lock the phone or computer so that nobody can access it; or, click Remote Wipe. Selecting Remote Wipe will remove all your personal data and settings from your computer or device and restore it to its factory setting.

FIGURE 8-2 Find your Mac, iPhone, or other device using the iCloud service.

4. To play a sound, click that tab and check that Play Sound is switched to On. Click Send to activate the alert sound. You can also type a message if you want, but you must click Send to either start the alert or send a message. If you opt to include a message, you might want to leave a phone number so the good Samaritan who found your device can call you.

 If you don't have location services enabled for your computer or device, you won't be able to use the Find My ... feature.

Control AutoSave and Versions

Once you get the hang of how they work, AutoSave and Versions are two particularly helpful features offered in Lion and Mountain Lion. With no effort at all on your part, your work is automatically saved without slowing you down or interrupting you. In Mountain Lion, you can save your document to iCloud. At present, AutoSave and Versions are only available with TextEdit and Preview or the apps in the iWork suite of applications (Pages, Keynote, and Numbers) if you purchased one or all of these. The examples shown in this section are illustrated with TextEdit.

Understand AutoSave and Versions

The days of compulsively pressing COMMAND-S are behind you. With AutoSave, any work you do is automatically saved every five minutes or when there is a pause in your work. The only time you need to employ the Save command is when you first name your TextEdit document and assign it a location (or in certain situations with Versions, which is explained in the next section). You can use AutoSave without even really thinking about it. With Mountain Lion, you have the option of saving your document to your free iCloud storage account. In order to save to iCloud, you must have already signed in to iCloud on your Mac with your Apple ID. To do so, click System Preferences, click iCloud, and then enter your Apple ID and password.

To give AutoSave a try, open TextEdit and type a few lines. When you want to name the file, do the following:

1. Press COMMAND-S to name your file.
2. Enter a name for your document over the highlighted text.
3. Select where you want to save the document from the pop-up menu. In Mountain Lion, iCloud is the default location, but you can choose other locations on your Mac.
4. Click Save.

After you perform this first simple step, you don't need to save the document again; it will all happen behind the scenes. Furthermore, every hour your Mac will save a version of your document in its current state. This means that you get several versions of your document at varying stages of progress. Rather than save multiple documents, you can access all of the versions in one document. For example, say you are working on a proposal and had several paragraphs of text that you typed early on, but deleted later in a fit of editorial pique. Later, if you decide those paragraphs were actually quite good and you want to resurrect them, you can access them through Versions. You can also copy and paste sections from one version to another or revert your document to an earlier stage.

Work with Versions in TextEdit

In order to work with Versions, you need to either work in the document for a while or save versions manually while you work—which may be a good idea if you type very quickly. To create versions before your Mac does each hour, press COMMAND-S from the File menu in TextEdit. The whole file isn't saved each time, only the changes since the last version. After you've worked on the document for a while and want to browse through Versions, do the following:

1. Point your cursor at the title bar at the top of TextEdit. An arrow will appear next to the title. Click the arrow and select Browse All Versions from the pop-up menu. You will automatically go to a screen that looks a lot like the starry backdrop for Time Machine.
2. Once you're in the Versions screen, the most current version of your document is on the left and a stack of earlier versions display on the right (see Figure 8-3). Click the title bar of each version in the stack to browse through earlier versions. You can also click through the timeline on the right to view your document at a certain period of time.
3. If you find an earlier version that you prefer to the current version and want to work from that, click Restore while that version is displayed at the top of the stack.
4. If you want to resurrect only a portion of an earlier version, you can copy and paste the text from that version to your current version. Find the portion of text that you want to move to your current version, and then highlight it and press COMMAND-C. Move your cursor to your current version and press COMMAND-V.
5. If you want to delete one of the versions while in the Versions screen, point your cursor at the title bar of that version and wait for an arrow to appear. Click the arrow and select Delete This Version.
6. Click Done when you are finished working in Versions.

Tip   If you make changes to the current version while in the Versions screen (for example, copying and pasting), when you click Done, the title will display with the word "Edited." Until the next Save, you will be unable to access the Versions screen. To work around this, type a few characters and press COMMAND-S.

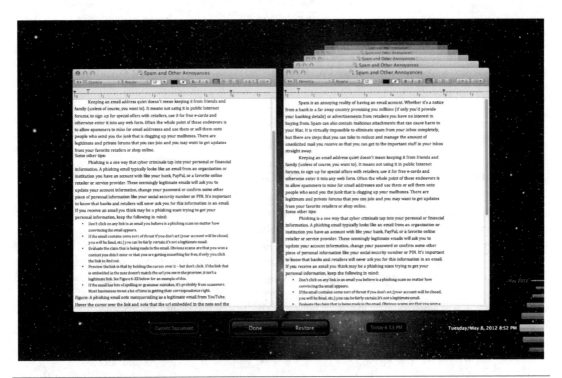

FIGURE 8-3 Your current document in Versions is on the left side of the screen and a stack of previous versions display on the right.

Rename a Version of Your Document

The Rename command added to Mountain Lion (you won't have this command if you still have Lion) allows you to change the title of your current document. You may want to employ this when you have a final version of your document or if you want to differentiate the current version from the previous. To rename your current document, do the following:

1. Point to the title in the title bar to get the arrow. When it appears, click it and select the Rename command. The text in the title will become highlighted.
2. Type over the existing title to rename your file and then press RETURN. The only versions with the new name will be the current one, and any subsequent versions that you save are saved automatically in Mountain Lion. Previous versions will have the old name but still be kept together in the same stack when you browse them in the Versions screen.

Lock a Document or Create a Duplicate in Versions

When you finish your masterpiece in TextEdit, you can lock it to prevent changes and also to prevent new versions from being created. Point your cursor at the title of your work and wait for the arrow to appear, and then select Lock from the pop-up menu. Once you lock the document, any time you try to edit it the window shown here appears. If you want to continue to edit it, click Unlock in this screen to resume your work and continue creating versions of the document as you work.

If you want to create a new document based on the work you have in a current version of your document, you can select the Duplicate command from the title bar. Point your cursor at the title, wait for the arrow to appear, and then select Duplicate from the pop-up menu. You can rename the file if you want and save it to a new location.

Finally, you can move your document to a different folder on your computer. If you want to refile your document somewhere else on your computer, point your cursor at the title bar to display the arrow. Select the Move To command and select a location to move your file to. This option is only available in Mountain Lion.

Fix Backward Scrolling

You scroll up, and the screen goes down! One of the bigger changes that Apple introduced in Lion was the addition of Multi-Touch gestures, including the inclusion of so-called natural scrolling. Some users love it, and you may already have the hang of it, but if you work on Windows or an older Mac OS X, you may find it difficult to switch back and forth between scrolling directions. Follow these steps to change the scrolling direction back to the same settings as in your earlier OS X:

1. Go to the Apple menu and select System Preferences.
2. Click Trackpad.
3. Clear the check box next to Scroll direction: natural (see Figure 8-4).
4. Close the window.

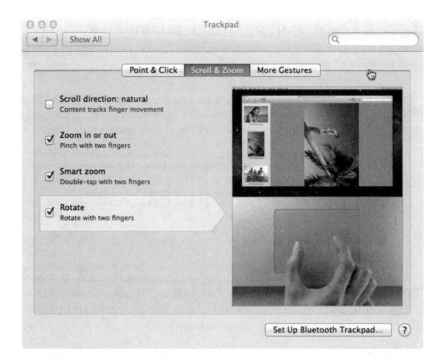

FIGURE 8-4 Change the scrolling direction of your trackpad or mouse to the way it was in previous releases of OS X.

Use or Disable Resume

When working in some apps like Word or Safari, you may have noticed that each time you launch the application, windows you had open when you quit the app automatically reopen. In fact, not only are the documents opened exactly as you left them, but also the cursor is where you left it, and any chunk of text you highlighted will remain so. Depending on how you work, this is either wonderful or something of an annoyance. On the one hand, you don't have to dig to find your recent work, and if you accidentally quit a program, you can simply launch it again and have all the windows you were currently working on reopen automatically. However, if you simply want to create a brand-new document, it can be a little annoying to have three old documents suddenly pop up on your desktop as well.

You have two choices if you want to disable Resume: you can disable it in all the applications that do this or disable just one app at a time. To disable it in all applications, open System Preferences and click General. Next, deselect the check box next to Restore windows when quitting and re-opening apps, as shown here.

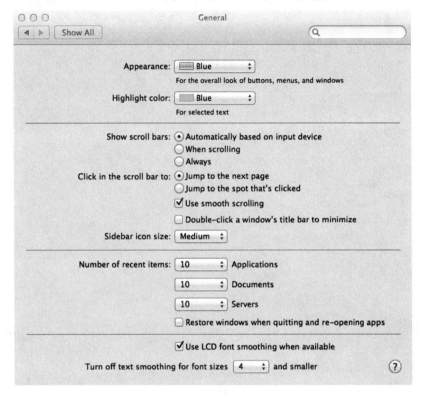

To disable this in one application, hold down the option key and then select Quit from the menu. A new command displays: Quit and Close All Windows. Select it to close all the windows open in the application. The next time you open the app, you'll be starting from a clean slate.

9 Secure Your Mac

Securing your Mac and all the important files you have on it is one of the most basic steps you can take to keep your computer healthy, but it's also something that many users overlook. A Mac with no security features enabled, even one in a home, can fall victim to an inexperienced user, a clueless visitor—or worse. All your files, personal information, Internet history, and passwords are instantly available as soon as someone turns on a Mac with no protection in place. If you leave the house with your MacBook, the security situation becomes even more perilous. In this chapter we'll look at some of the many ways you can keep others out of your personal data by enabling some of Apple's ready-made security and privacy features, including disabling automatic login, creating user accounts, and enabling the firewall and FileVault.

Configure Security & Privacy Settings

Your Mac comes with many features to protect your data and privacy. In this next section we look at many of the basic features that you can enable with just a few clicks, including password-protecting your screen saver, disabling automatic login, and enabling the firewall.

Protect Your Mac with a Password for Sleep and Screen Saver

We've all stepped away from our Mac for "just a minute," only to have that minute stretch into a much longer period of time. While you are away from your computer, anyone can access your personal files or otherwise cause some sort of mischief to your Mac. Requiring a password to wake your Mac from sleep, if you've been gone for quite a while, or when a screen saver is running, prevents others from snooping around your user account when you step away from your computer.

1. Open System Preferences from the Apple menu and click Security & Privacy.
2. Click the General button.
3. Select the check box next to Require password for sleep and screen saver, and then select a time frame from the pop-up menu. The default password will be the login password for the current user.

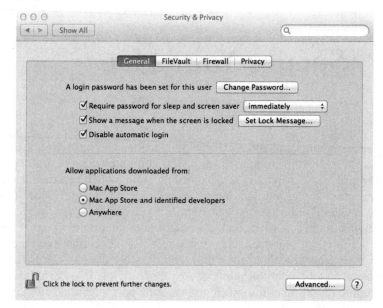

Your Mac goes to sleep by default after 10 minutes of inactivity. If you want to change it so that it will sleep sooner, you can configure this in System Preferences by clicking Energy Saver and moving the slide bar for Computer Sleep to 5 minutes—or some other time frame.

Tip   If you want the screen saver to launch as soon as you get up from your computer, configure a Hot Corner to start this automatically. Choose System Preferences from the Apple menu, and then click Desktop & Screen Saver. Click the Screen Saver button and click Hot Corners. Click one of the pop-up windows that corresponds to one of the corners on your Mac's display, and select Start Screen Saver. The next time you get ready to step away from your Mac, park your cursor in the corner to launch the screen saver. You can disable the screen saver when you return by entering your password.

Disable Automatic Login

As convenient as it may be to launch directly to your home screen when your Mac starts up, it's not terrifically safe. If your Mac is lost or stolen, or if someone gains access to your computer while you are away from it, they will be able to access everything on your Macintosh HD. Always be certain that automatic login is disabled, and require a login password for all user accounts (user accounts will be explored more in "Create and Manage User Accounts"). To disable automatic login, open System Preferences from the Apple menu, and then click Security & Privacy. Click the General button, and then select the check box next to Disable automatic login.

Enable the Firewall

Firewall is Apple's security application that helps monitor the exchange of data over an Internet connection. Applications regularly need permission to use the Internet, and with the Mac Firewall enabled, you can specify which applications can send information back and forth to your Mac. Most routers (the piece of hardware that broadcasts your wireless signal) have a firewall enabled. We'll explore more about networks, routers, and the like in the next chapter. In the meantime, you should enable your firewall if you use your MacBook while you are out and make use of public Wi-Fi networks, or if your router doesn't have a firewall enabled. You might also consider running Firewall all the time to minimize the risks of attack from other computers on the network. Do the following to enable Firewall on your Mac:

1. Click System Preferences in the Dock or select System Preferences from the Apple menu, and then click Security & Privacy.
2. Click the Firewall tab at the top of the window. If the window is locked, click the padlock symbol and enter your password when prompted.
3. Click Turn On Firewall, and then click Firewall Options. In the window, there are three options you can configure depending on what you want from the firewall. Select the check box next to the feature you want to enable. In most cases, you won't want to use the first option to block all incoming connections, as this may prevent you from utilizing some basic features of your Mac, like Mail and Safari.

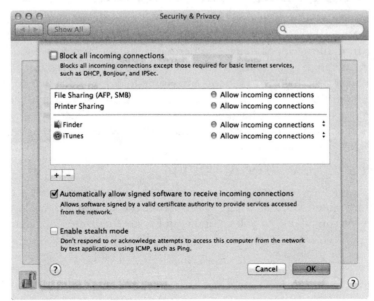

- **Block all incoming connections** This is the most restrictive option and will block file sharing and connections you need for certain applications, and you may lose the ability to "see" other computers on your network. If you want the maximum security, especially while you are away from a secure home or business network, you could enable this option.
- **Automatically allow signed software to receive incoming connections** Signed software includes applications that are confirmed by third-party certificates to be authentic companies. If you have an application that you want to allow to receive incoming connections, you can click the plus (+) symbol and then navigate to Applications and add it to the list of allowed connections. Alternatively, you can click the minus (–) symbol to include applications you want to block from sending connections to your Mac.
- **Stealth Mode** Your Mac won't respond to requests from unknown computers asking to send data to you. Hackers often send out automated requests to computers looking for a response so they can determine whether a computer is turned on and connected to the Internet. Stealth Mode protects you by not responding to these messages, effectively hiding your Mac from others—some of whom are interested in accessing your computer to spam you, hijack your computer, or cause some other sort of damage.

 One downside of enabling Stealth Mode when you're at home is being unable to use Ping to test your Mac's connectivity.

After you've enabled the options you want for Firewall, click OK.

Create and Manage User Accounts

Creating and using separate user accounts and passwords for each individual who uses your Mac is vital to keeping your Mac secure. User accounts protect data and system files from the accidental havoc sometimes wrought by novice users. User accounts also offer each individual a fair bit of privacy. Once the user accounts have been created, each user gets their own desktop and Home folder with the accompanying files like Documents, Music and Pictures, as well as the ability to customize many of their preferences if they are assigned a Standard account. There are other types of accounts you can configure for users of your Mac, which we explore in more detail next.

Create New User Accounts

If there is only one user account on your Mac at present, that account is the Administrator account. When you first set up your brand-new Mac, you entered a password and name so you could log in for the first time. This name and password belong to the Administrator (you!), and you'll need them to add and manage accounts for other users. As an Administrator, you have the power to install new applications, change System Preferences, and access and edit other users' files as well as manage your Mac's network (which is explored more in the next chapter). Here are descriptions of other types of user accounts:

- **Standard**   A Standard user gets their own home folder and can manage many of the preferences for their own account including customizing the way their display and Finder look and function. Any files that the user creates are their own to modify or delete as they see fit. Standard users can install software for that user account.
- **Managed with Parental Controls**   You can use this type of account for an inexperienced user or young children. Administrators can provide a simplified Finder, limit what applications the user can access, what apps they can use, what sites they visit on the Internet, and who the user sends messages to as well as limiting the amount of time spent on the computer.
- **Sharing Only**   This type of user can only log in over a network, not directly from the Mac. You can place files you want to share in a specific location on your Mac so that Sharing Only users can access them. Depending on the permissions you set for this user, you can prevent them from making changes or enable them to make changes to the files.
- **Group**   A group is a collection of accounts that share certain things in common. By applying this option to user accounts, you can create or limit shared resources to users in the group at the same time rather than managing permissions in each individual account.
- **Guest**   This isn't a type of account you can create, but it will be there by default in the login screen of your Mac. If you have a friend or visiting family member who wants to use your computer and won't need to store any files, you can have them log in with the Guest account. Once a user logs out of the Guest account, any files or other changes made to the account are deleted.

To add a new user account, you need to select System Preferences from the Apple menu and click the Users & Groups icon. Once you're in the Users & Groups window, do the following:

1. Click the padlock symbol, type in the Admin password, and then click Unlock.
2. Click the plus (+) symbol.

3. Select a user account type from the pop-up menu (Standard, Managed, Sharing-only, and so forth). You can go back and change the account type if you want to change it later.

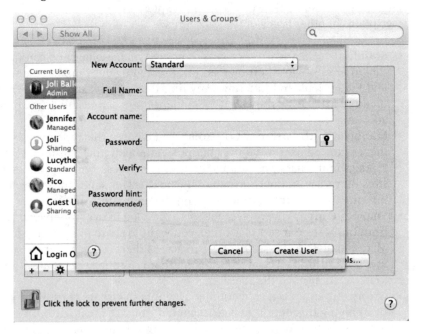

4. Enter the account user's full name in the first box and then an account name in the second. The account name is what will display next to the user's home folder and is usually a shorter version of someone's name by default. You can also enter a nickname for the user, like Jude for Judith and so forth.

5. Enter a password for the user and then verify the password in the next box.

6. Type a hint that will help jog your memory in case you forget their password. Share it with the user so that when they log in, they can then create their own strong password that the Administrator doesn't know. A strong password is one that can't be easily guessed and contains a combination of letters, numbers, and symbols.

7. Enter the Apple ID for the user if they have one. This will enable them to access features like iTunes and the App Store (if they are a Standard user).

8. To add a photo to the user account, click the default Apple image and select Edit Picture. You can find an image on your Mac or take a photo if your computer has a camera attached.

9. Click the padlock symbol when you are done, to prevent anyone from making changes without your permission.

You can switch between user accounts quickly by using the Fast User Switching option in the context menu. In the upper-right corner of your screen, you should see the current user name. Click the user name and a list of users appears beneath it as

FIGURE 9-1   Switch quickly between user accounts with just a password.

shown in Figure 9-1. Select the user whose account you want to switch to, enter the user account password when prompted, and you will be switched to the account. This option is handy if one user wants to log in quickly to their account while the other is working. Nobody has to close up their work or go through the logout process.

If you don't see a user name in your menu, you can go into System Preferences and enable this option in the Users & Groups window. Once you're in Users & Groups, click Login Options. You may be prompted to unlock the padlock and enter the Administrator's password. Next, select the check box next to Show fast user switching, and select an option from the pop-up menu. You can choose from Full Name, Short Name, or User Icon.

Each time you switch back and forth between user accounts, you'll need to enter the user's password. If one user logs out, the other will still be logged in. Remember to log everyone out before you shut down the Mac.

Tip   If you forgot one of the user's passwords, you can go into the Users & Groups window and click Reset Password. You can start from scratch rather than having to enter the old, forgotten password.

Consider Changing Your Account to Standard for Added Security

Even if you are the resident computer guru in your home, you can still expose your Mac to additional security risks if you log in with an Administrator's account each time you use your computer. Malware accidentally downloaded on an Admin account has the potential to do more damage than on a Standard account. If you make some accidental changes to your Mac OS X that cause it to work improperly (or not at all), you won't have an Administrator's account to log in to to sort the problem out. When you work in a Standard account, you can still make use of the Administrator's password when needed. When you need to install new software or upgrades, you can log in as the Administrator to perform these functions.

(continued)

Rather than start from scratch and create a whole new account and reconfigure all your personal preferences, you can simply change your present account to a Standard account—after first creating a new Administrator's account. Start by doing the following to create a new Admin account:

1. Go the Apple menu, select System Preferences, and then click Users & Groups.
2. Click the padlock and enter the Admin password when prompted.
3. Click the plus (+) symbol to create a new account. Select Administrator from the pop-up menu and enter your full name and account name. You can use some variation of your name or simply label the account Admin.
4. Enter a password twice and leave yourself a hint in the box.
5. Click the padlock symbol to preserve the changes.
6. Log out of your present account and log in to the new Administrator's account.
7. Select System Preferences from the Apple menu, and then click Users & Groups.
8. Unlock the padlock, and then click your previous Admin account. Deselect the check box next to Allow this user to administer this computer. You should see the account type change to Standard beneath your account name.
9. Lock the padlock symbol again to keep the changes, and then log back in to your Standard account to continue working.

Configure Parental Controls

Apple offers an excellent feature that allows you to manage what content your users can access on the Internet, how they use the Mac, and whom they chat with. Limiting access to certain sites not only protects children from inappropriate content; it can also prevent users from visiting sites that may contain malicious software, and it is another great way to keep your Mac secure. You might also want to consider configuring Parental Controls if you have a very inexperienced user working on your computer as well.

If you already have a Standard user account for your novice user, you can simply switch it to a Parental Control account by clicking the user name in the list on the left of the Users & Groups window and then selecting the check box next to Enable parental controls.

Parental Controls come with several possible controls that cover the types of applications the user can access, what sites they can visit on the Internet, who they can communicate with in Mail and Messages, how long they can spend on the computer each day, and whether they can change the settings for things like their own password or printer configurations (see Figure 9-2). What you decide to enable or restrict depends on the user you have in mind. Several of the possible configurations you can make to a user account with a mind toward keeping your Mac secure are discussed next.

FIGURE 9-2   Limit users' access to applications in the Parental Controls window.

In the Apps window of Parental Controls, you can manage the applications the user can access. First, select the check box next to Limit Applications. After you enable this, you can click the arrow next to Allow App Store Apps and deselect any apps you want to limit. You can also allow App Store apps based on age range by clicking the pop-up menu and selecting an appropriate age range for a young user. For example, if you have a game that has a 17+ rating, you can limit your young child from playing it by selecting 4+ from the pop-up menu.

To restrict access to certain web sites, click the Web tab at the top of the Parental Controls window. Select the check box next to Try to limit access to adult web sites automatically. A really determined user may be able to get around these restrictions, but you can at least slow down their access by enabling this option. You can add to the list of forbidden web sites by clicking the Customize button and adding specific sites you want to block. Click the plus symbol beneath Never allow these web sites, and type in the URL, as shown next. Conversely, you can add sites that the user can access by clicking the plus (+) symbol beneath Always allow these web sites. When you have finished adding or limiting pages, click OK.

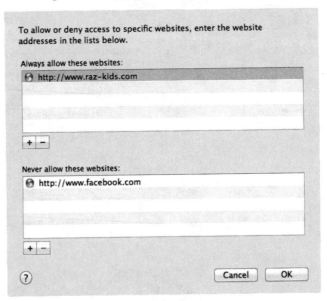

You have one additional option to restrict web sites that is especially good if the user is a child. Selecting the radio button next to Allow access only to these web sites limits the number of web sites your child can visit to those listed in the box. You can add to the list by clicking the plus (+) symbol and entering a URL. While selecting this is the most restrictive option, it is one way to ensure that your user (and Mac) stay safe.

Tip If you want to know what web sites your managed users have visited, you can click Logs at the bottom of the Parental Controls window. When you click this, you are taken to a list of the recent sites the user visited, among other things. If you see a specific site that you are concerned about, you can add that to the blocked list. Logs are also available for applications and people they've communicated with in Messages and Mail.

If you are concerned about who the user is communicating with and their activities in Game Center, you can exercise some control over these activities as well, as shown in the next illustration. To limit the contacts your user can communicate with, select the check boxes next to Limit Mail and Limit Messages. Next, click the plus symbol beneath Allowed Contacts and enter the email addresses of individuals you know and trust. You can also have the application send you a request for permission to add a contact by selecting the check box next to Send permission request to and entering your email address. If you want to limit the user from joining multiplayer games in Game Center or restrict adding Game Center friends, clear those check boxes at the top of the window.

Finally, use Parental Controls to prevent the user from changing their password in the Users & Groups window. Click Other at the top of Parental Controls and select the check box next to Disable changing the password.

Encrypt Your Data with FileVault

FileVault encrypts all the data on your Macintosh HD including system files, user files, and applications. After you log out of your account, the data on your disk will be unreadable to anyone who doesn't have the encryption key (a type of password). Each time you create a new file, FileVault encrypts the data, and no one but the Administrator or someone with the password can unlock it. Access to your encrypted data is dependent on a password generated by the application. If you worry about what would happen to your computer if it was stolen or someone else accessed it, FileVault may be an application you want to use. Remember that you'll need all the passwords for all of your user accounts.

One potential drawback to enabling FileVault is the risk of losing your encryption password. If you forget or misplace the password, your data will be permanently locked and you'll need to wipe your Macintosh HD and start from scratch.

To set up FileVault on your Mac:

1. Select System Preferences from the Apple menu, and then click Security & Privacy.
2. Click the padlock and enter your password when prompted.
3. Click Turn On FireVault. When the list of account users appears, click Enable User for each user you trust with the ability to unlock your Mac and type in their passwords when prompted. If a user isn't enabled, they can't log in to their account until another user or the administrator has unlocked the Mac with the key. When you have finished, click Continue.

4. The next screen you see displays the recovery key, as shown in Figure 9-3. It is essential that you print out the key or copy it down and physically put it somewhere safe (and where you'll remember it). If you lose the key, you will be unable to unlock your computer and all the data for all your users will be lost. Click Continue after you record the key.
5. You can choose to store your recovery key with Apple. In the window that appears, select the radio button next to Store the recovery key with Apple, and then click Continue. Select three security questions from the pop-up boxes and enter the answers beneath each question. Click Continue after you enter the responses to all three security questions.

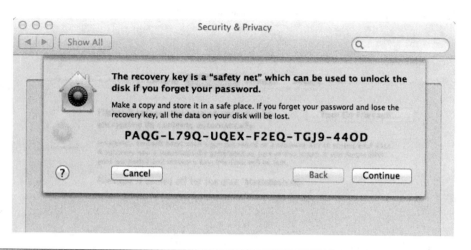

FIGURE 9-3   The recovery key to FileVault, which you need to unlock your encrypted Macintosh if you forget your password

6. Click the Restart button when prompted. When your Mac starts up again, you can log in again and work normally while FileVault encrypts your disk. You should see the FireVault window in Preferences on your desktop with a progress bar showing how far the along the encryption process is. Encrypting an entire Macintosh HD can take many hours. The first time is the longest, and subsequent files you create will be encrypted as you create them and will take less time.

Note   FileVault requires OS X Lion or Mountain Lion and Recovery HD on your Mac's startup drive. If for some reason Recovery HD could not be installed, you will be unable to use FileVault.

Remember that your disk is encrypted when you log out of your account each time. If you have very sensitive information on your Macintosh HD, you may want to log out of your account each time you step away from your computer rather than just using a password to wake your Mac from sleep or from a screen saver. When you go to log in again, you will need your password to unlock your account.

If you forget or misplace your encryption key and if you opted to store it with Apple, you can contact AppleCare and ask to retrieve it. You'll need to remember the answers to all three of your security questions and have your computer's details available (serial number and record number).

10   Secure Your Network

Your network allows you to connect your Mac to other computers, to the Internet through a cable modem or DSL, and to other hardware like scanners, printers, and backup drives. Having all these connections is hugely convenient and something most of us take for granted as part of using our Macs. However, all of this convenience brings with it risks to the security of our data and the health of our Macs. A poorly configured wireless network, for example, can broadcast everything you submit over the network—including important personal or financial information. This chapter looks at the ways you can protect your network by changing some of the default security settings on your network hardware and by configuring safer file sharing with others on the network.

Explore Your Current Hardware Setup

Your hardware setup will vary slightly depending on how many computers or devices you have connected, and whether you have a wired (Ethernet) or wireless network. At the very least, you probably have a router that connects everything on your network. Many of the words used to describe network hardware are used interchangeably to describe similar things, like switches or hubs. All this generalization can make it hard to figure out exactly what you have. If you're not sure about what types of hardware to look for, review some of the basics listed here to help you identify what you have for your network.

- **Ethernet router**   Contains jacks that can connect several Macs, devices, and a DSL or cable modem. Most Macs come with an Ethernet jack to connect to the main Ethernet router (or hub). A typical home router contains a built-in switch which will have four or five jacks (or more) to plug in the cables that connect your network.
- **Hub or switch**   Both act as the central point to connect computers and devices on your network. You need a router, a switch, or a hub to connect your devices and computers. A *hub* takes whatever is received over the network (file, image, and so on) and transmits it to all computers on the network (though only the intended device can actually receive it). A *switch* is a smarter version of a hub—it directs network traffic between computers, for example, by sending data only from one computer to another. If possible, you should always opt for a switch, or an Ethernet router with a built-in switch, to maximize your network's efficiency and security.

- **Wireless router** Broadcasts your network to other computers and devices in your home. It is connected to a cable modem or DSL and your Mac. Your devices need to be within 150 feet or so of the wireless router to pick up the Internet connection and see other devices on the network. Some routers have external antennas that stick out the top of the box.
- **Apple devices** You may have an Apple wireless router like an AirPort Extreme, AirPort Express, or Time Capsule that connects the devices and computers over your Wi-Fi network.

Ethernet networks will have several cables connecting centrally through the router. Wireless networks connect via cable from the cable modem or DSL to the wireless router and also to your Mac.

Are Cables and Routers Physically Secure?

An important but often overlooked security step to protect your network is ensuring that both your routers and cables aren't exposed in any way. This serves a few important functions. First, with Ethernet networks, keeping routers out of easy reach prevents others in your home or small office from accidentally disconnecting the network or interfering with the hardware in some other way. For example, many routers come with a reset option that you can invoke by holding down a button on the router. Keeping your hardware secure also prevents anyone from plugging in to the network (with a device or computer) without your knowledge, either innocently or in an attempt to deliberately attack your network. The same is true for wireless networks; the more easily accessed your router, the greater the potential for accidental or deliberate mischief to your network. At a minimum, make sure your routers and cables are kept reasonably out of the way of household (or office) activity and traffic.

Choose Between Wi-Fi and Ethernet

When you're presented with a choice between Ethernet or Wi-Fi, choose Ethernet as you'll get a faster and more secure connection. Wireless networks carry a bigger security risk because, with the right set of tools, someone who is not a user in your network can watch your network traffic and even join your network. This is especially true of poorly configured home networks. However, you should use wireless networks when Ethernet connections are difficult or impossible to set up. If you have an iOS device, you can create a wireless part of the network for that.

Inventory Passwords for Your Network

You must use passwords to secure your network against intrusion. You'll already have a default password for your router (provided by the manufacturer) and may also have a password for the administrative interface for your router. If you are still using the default passwords assigned by the manufacturer, you should change those and create new, strong passwords with a combination of numbers, upper- and lowercase letters and symbols, and at least eight characters long. The longer the password, the more difficult it will be to crack.

Change Security Settings on Your Router

You can change the security settings of most non-Apple routers through Safari or another browser. However, before you can change the security settings, you need to locate the router's IP address. The address usually consists of several numbers separated by periods, like 192.168.1.254. You can look for the IP address on the router itself or with the paperwork that came with the router when you bought it. Once you locate the address, type it directly into your URL bar, as shown in Figure 10-1.

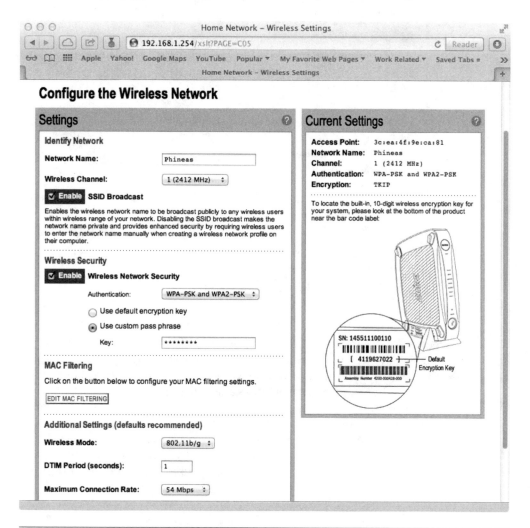

FIGURE 10-1   Security settings page for a router

The directions for your router will vary depending on the manufacturer and service provider. To improve the security of your wireless network, do the following:

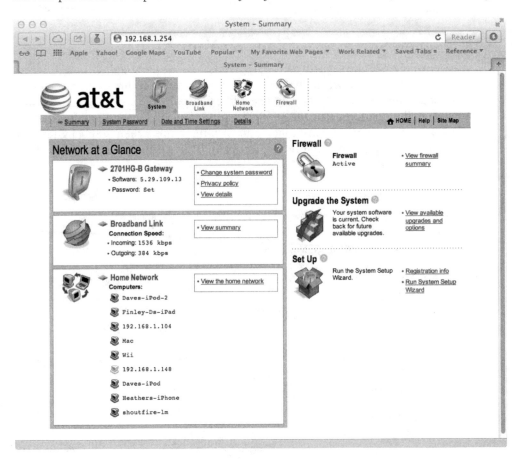

- **Confirm that the firewall is turned on** The router's firewall protects your network from unauthorized access or attack. Most routers will have the firewall enabled by default, but you should check this yourself.
- **Change the default administrative name and password** When you install a router, the manufacturer provides a default administrative user name and password and sometimes a user name. The administrator name can sometimes be simply "admin," and the default password is usually one that isn't very secure (to help you set up quickly). In fact, many hackers are aware of the default names and passwords for well-known routers and, if you haven't done so already, you should change the admin name and password to keep your network from falling prey to hackers.

- **Change the wireless network password**   The wireless network password is the one that others use to join your wireless network. This password usually acts as the encryption key as well. If you didn't do so when you first set it up, change the router password from the one set by the manufacturer, which is often just a string of numbers. The new password should be one that is difficult to guess and includes letters, numbers, and symbols.
- **Change your SSID (network name)**   The SSID is the name that displays when your Mac or devices "look" for a wireless network. If you have an AirPort Base Station, its default SSID is usually Apple Network followed by several digits. If you have a different router, the network name is one assigned by the manufacturer. For example, if you have a 2WIRE router, the default network name might be 2WIRE123 or some combination of the manufacturer name and numbers. Hackers or snoops who see a network broadcasting the default SSID will know they are looking at a poorly configured network, and may try to attack it. Create a network name that is easy for you to remember and one that won't be easily mixed up with your neighbor's SSID. Avoid using personal information like birthdates or family names when you create a new network name.
- **Check the encryption type**   Most routers offer encryption options so that the data you send while on the wireless network will be unintelligible to anyone who doesn't have the key. The key is usually the same password you use to join a network. There are a few types of encryption protocol, but the two most common types are WEP and WPA. Of the two, WPA is more secure. When you are in the security settings for your router, check that WPA is selected. WEP has long been shown to be easy to crack and offers very little real protection. Despite the obvious problems with WEP, some routers are still set to WEP by default.

Note   You may have older hardware that doesn't function with WPA. If this is the case, update your hardware as soon as possible to ensure that you can apply the safest encryption methods to your router.

- **Consider hiding your SSID**   You can "hide" your network name and prevent it from being broadcast and viewed by any passersby. A hidden SSID can still be accessed, but users will need to type in the network name manually. There is some debate about whether disabling the SSID broadcast has much of an effect on network security, and there are drawbacks to doing this. For example, it can make it more difficult for users to join the network as their Mac won't "see" your network as an option in the menu. If there are only a few users on your network, it may be a good option. To hide your network from strangers, select the "hide" option on the administrative screen of your router or deselect SSID Broadcast, depending on the settings. While enabling this option can deter casual attackers, it won't have much of an effect on someone determined to target your network.

If you have Apple AirPort Express, AirPort Extreme, or Time Capsule, you can configure many of the same security settings for your device in Airport Utility. Open Launchpad and click AirPort Utility, and then change the Wireless Network Name. Once you make the changes and click Update, your base station will restart.

Reconfigure the Position of the Wi-Fi Router

You may have initially placed your wireless access point where it was most convenient, perhaps immediately next to your computer or in an office in your home. While keeping in mind that you should keep it somewhere it can't be easily interfered with, make sure it's placed so that it broadcasts to as much of your home as you need it to (for example, within range of all your computers and devices). All of this is easier said than done, however, and you may have to experiment with different positions to find the one that works best for your home or apartment. Other considerations to keep in mind when placing your Wi-Fi router:

- Place the access point in a central location to reach as much of your home as you need.
- Turn down the transmit power to as low a level as still provides adequate coverage.
- Avoid putting the router behind walls, bookshelves, and filing cabinets.
- Keep the router away from other home appliances that send signals, like wireless telephones, baby monitors, and some microwaves.

Configure More Secure Sharing

There are a number of ways to share over your network. You can share printers and other devices and also files and folders. To preserve the health of your Mac, you should keep close tabs on what you share and how you configure the sharing options. The more widely you share files and folders on your Mac, the less secure your data will be. In this next section we'll focus on how to share files and folder more securely.

Review What's Currently Shared

You may already have sharing enabled and regularly use your Public folder to allow others on your network access to select files or folders. There are other ways to share data, too. For example, you can share a single file or folder from anywhere on your Mac without dragging it to your Public folder. If you don't have sharing enabled, you can do that now by opening System Preferences, clicking Sharing, and then clicking the radio button next to File Sharing. It will turn green to show it's on. Make note of services you have enabled by looking at the check boxes next to the services on the left. You can share a number of resources on your network, but this section will focus on the most common type of sharing—files and folders between Macs on a network (we'll look more at sharing your network with a PC in Chapter 11).

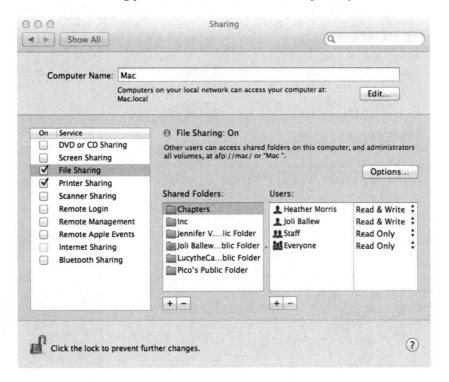

Tip	You can access the Sharing Folder in Preferences quickly by CONTROL-clicking the System Preferences icon in the Dock and then selecting Sharing.

Once you are in the Sharing window, you'll see the Public folders of all the users on that Mac as well as any folders that you've shared on the network, under the heading "Shared Folders." To the right of the folder list are all the users that are currently enabled to share the selected folder. Next to the users is the level of access (privileges) each is allowed for a particular folder. The types of privileges include:

- **Read Only**   Others can look at the contents of the folder but can't make changes or delete content in them.
- **Read & Write**   Users with this level of privilege can read, change, and even delete a file in the folder. You are assigned Read & Write access by default for the folders on your user account (as well as each of the user accounts on your Mac). There are a few circumstances where you might grant this level of privilege to other users, but in general, you should only grant Read permissions to others.
- **Write Only (Drop Box)**   Allows others to add a file to a shared folder, but they can't access or see what is in that folder.

You can change or edit the permissions for shared folders at any time in the Sharing window in System Preferences. For example, if you see that you have a folder where everyone has Read & Write privileges, you can select Read only from the pop-up menu in the Users window. You can also add new folders to share in this window by clicking the plus (+) symbol under the Shared Folders list and navigating to a folder on your Mac you want to share. You can also configure sharing through the Get Info window, which we'll explore next.

Configure More Secure Sharing

Choosing a specific file or folder to share without moving it to the Public folder is a good idea for a few reasons. It's better than sharing your entire Macintosh HD and easier than dragging files to the Public folder. To keep your Mac secure, opt for Read permissions for most users. You can also limit access to individual users, rather than everyone, and grant access only after they've supplied a password.

To share a document or folder:

1. Select the document or folder by clicking it once, and then press COMMAND-I or choose Get Info from the File menu.
2. Select the check box next to Shared folder (see Figure 10-2).
3. Click Sharing & Permissions to expand the window. You may need to unlock the window and enter your admin password. Under the headings Name and Privilege, the users on your network display on the left and permissions on the right. Your name appears at the top as well as "staff" and "everyone."
4. Set the permissions for each of the users you want to share the document or folder with. There is also an option for "everyone," and that is "No access." This means that others on the network won't be able to see the file.

FIGURE 10-2 Create a shared folder through the Get Info window.

5. If you want to create password-protected access for one specific user, click the plus (+) symbol beneath the list of names. A new window appears with a list of other users from Contacts. Scroll through the list to find the specific name, highlight it, and click Select. When prompted, create a password for the person and then click Create Account. The person's name will display in the Name column in Sharing & Permissions. Set access privileges for the person from the pop-up menu.

Choose Read permissions for most people on your network. If they want to edit a file in some way, they can make a duplicate of it and then make changes. This strategy works well if you have a template to share, but you want to ensure that nobody on the network makes changes to the original.

Use AirDrop When Applicable

AirDrop is a fast and secure way to share files with other Mac users running Lion or Mountain Lion who are on the same Wi-Fi network. You don't have to configure anything in your System Preferences—it's available when Wi-Fi is on and once you upgrade to Lion or Mountain Lion. When each person opens AirDrop, they'll see the picture or icon of the other user (see Figure 10-3). To share a file, you simply drag and drop the file onto the other user's icon. It's a good option because nobody can take files from your Mac—you have to push the file to them. You might consider using AirDrop when you want to share a file with someone that you *don't* want to network your Mac with. It's also fairly secure as the file is encrypted in transit so nobody else can decipher what is being sent. To use AirDrop:

1. Each user should open Finder and click AirDrop in the sidebar.
2. The sender drags a file or folder onto the icon of the recipient. When prompted, click Send. On the other Mac, the user will need to click Save and Open, Decline, or Save.
3. The recipient can access file in the Downloads folder in the Dock.

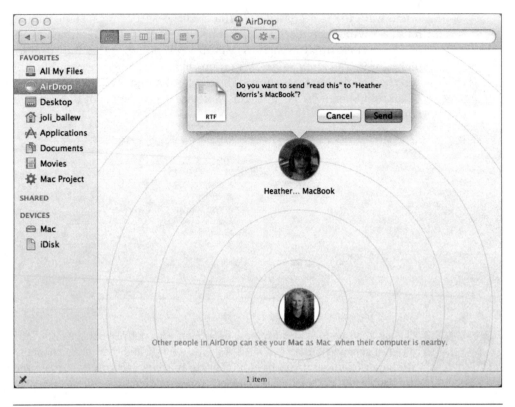

FIGURE 10-3   Use AirDrop to share files securely.

Not all Macs support AirDrop. Models that support this feature include MacBooks and MacBook Pros from late 2008, iMac from early 2009, Mac Minis from mid-2010, MacBook Air from late 2010, and all newer models after these.

11 Share Safely Between Your Mac and Windows PC

Many home and business networks contain a combination of Mac and Windows computers, and those computers may also have different versions of the operating systems installed on them. Sharing data among different operating systems and different computer manufacturers can be problematic, though, as you've likely already experienced. Thus, in this chapter you'll first learn how to share data and share it safely, no matter what kind of network you have, and then you'll learn how to resolve some of the problems you're still encountering (if you are).

> **Note** The steps for sharing files throughout this chapter are shown with OS X Mountain Lion and Windows 7 Home Premium. If you are using different operating systems on any of the computers, the steps will differ. If you are on an earlier version of Lion, you should update your OS X as soon as possible (or, better yet, upgrade to Mountain Lion) as there are several known problems with file sharing in the earlier versions of Lion.

Create User Accounts and Passwords

If you don't have them already, you'll need to set up user accounts on both your Mac and Windows PC in order to share selected folders effectively. Sharing between computers is done from user account to user account rather than from computer to computer. If you only have one user account for your PC, it's the administrator account and you should add a Standard account to share with—we'll show you how next. If you have user accounts and passwords for both your Mac and Windows PC, you can skip to the next section to start exploring sharing options.

> **Note** For information on how to create and manage user accounts on your Mac, see Chapter 9.

Create User Accounts on Your Windows PC

Creating user accounts on your Windows PC is an essential step in setting up shared resources over your network. You should create and use a Standard account for everyday computing to keep your computer safe. Regularly using an administrator puts your PC at greater risk. If a rogue virus, hacker, or other Internet intruder attacks your PC while you're logged on as a Standard user, for instance, at least that's all the access they'll have without asking for administrator credentials (in theory anyway!).

To create a Standard user account on your Window PC:

 If you're using Windows 8, you no longer have a Start button. When you want to go somewhere like Control Panel, you do so from the Start screen. Just type Control Panel there and choose from the results.

1. Click Start, then select Control Panel.
2. Click Add or remove user accounts, and then click Create a new account.
3. Enter a name for the user and check that the radio button for Standard user is selected. You can use just a first name or nickname here, but you can't use any punctuation.

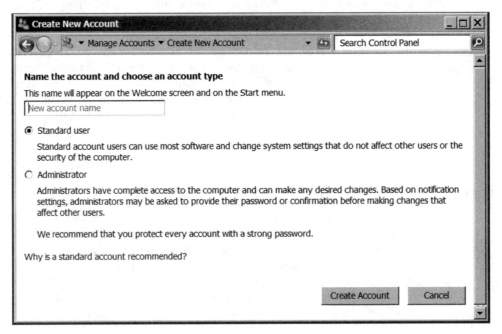

4. Click Create Account.

Tip
You can also add Parental Controls to new user accounts to help keep your Windows PC—and your extended network—safe from malware. Children are notorious for making a healthy computer unhealthy! To do this, in the Manage Accounts window, click the user's name, and then click Set up Parental Controls. Select the radio button next to On. Once you enable Parental Controls for a user account, you can allow or block the user from using specific programs. For example, if you have a young user on your Windows PC, you might block them from using Internet Explorer and prevent them from inadvertently downloading malware. If you do block IE, be sure to block other programs as well, like Firefox, Safari, Chrome, and other available browsers.

Create Passwords for User Accounts in Windows

To keep your Windows PC safe and to prevent unauthorized access to a user's account data, create strong passwords for each user in Windows. The user names and passwords you create here are what you'll need to access Windows files from your Mac, so keep track of them.

The best passwords consist of letters, both capitalized and not, numbers, and special characters. Unfortunately, when you create passwords like this, you have to keep them written down and handily available—which often poses a security problem in itself. Thus, when creating strong passwords, consider something you can remember, like this: MyDogHasFLEAS2012#.

To create a password for the new user account:

1. Click Start and select Control Panel, and then click Add or remove user accounts.
2. Click the icon of the user account you've just created, and then click Create a password.
3. Enter the password into the new password field and re-enter it to confirm. Leave a password hint if you want. A hint can help you remember the password if you forget, but it's not strictly necessary as the administrator can reset the password if needed.

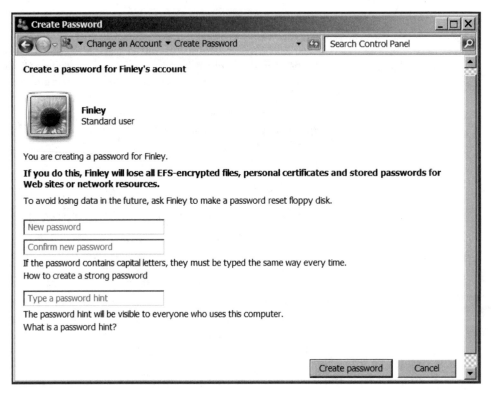

4. Click Create password.

 You may have noticed a warning about losing all EFS-encrypted files, personal certificates, and stored passwords for Web sites or network resources if you create a password. As long as the administrator creates a password for the new user right after creating the account, this shouldn't be a concern.

After you create one or more accounts with passwords, you can switch between them from the Start menu or access them from the logon screen. To switch accounts while in another user account, click the Start menu, click the arrow next to Shut down, and then select Switch user.

Explore Sharing Options

You can share files between your Mac and Windows computer(s) on your network in a few ways, including making use of the Public folders that are available to each user account, or by sharing a single folder over the network. You can even share an entire disk if you choose (but this is not something we recommend). In addition to sharing common items like documents, you can share printers, scanners, and even CD and DVD drives across the network.

- **Public**   On your Windows PC you have several public folders set up by default, including Documents, Downloads, Music, Pictures, and Videos. Once you enable Public folder sharing, anyone on your network can access the files you put there. On your Mac, each user has a Public file where they can drag folders and share them across the network. Using shared Public folders is a common way to safely share files on Windows computers, and can be part of a healthy network.
- **Share a Folder**   On your Windows PC you can enable sharing for a single folder and set permissions for it—in much the same way as you can with your Mac. You specify which users can access the folder and what level of access they have (Read or Read/Write in Windows).
- **Share Printers or Scanners**   You can share a printer or scanner across computers on your network. If you have a printer or scanner connected via USB to your Mac (rather than over Wi-Fi or Ethernet), you share them with the Windows PC on your network. Although this doesn't make your Mac healthier, it does improve the health of your pocketbook!
- **Share CD and DVD Drives**   If one of your computers doesn't have a CD or DVD drive, you can share the drive with the other computer and play media via your network.

Caution   File sharing is a common route for viruses to pass between computers. Both your Mac and Windows PC(s) should have malware protection in place in the form of anti-virus programs. Additionally, you should have these programs configured to scan for problems regularly. Many of the security tips discussed in Chapters 3 and 6 apply equally to your Windows PC.

Configure Sharing

Setting up sharing between a Mac and Windows PC on a network is fairly straightforward and can usually be achieved in a few clicks. We'll show you how to configure basic sharing on Windows and your Mac and also how to configure what to share, with whom, and how much access you might want to grant other users. This next section looks only at setting up these options, not accessing the files across computers, which we'll look at in more detail shortly.

Configure Sharing on Your Windows PC

Before you can get your Mac and Windows PC talking to each other, you need to enable some of the sharing features that are available on both. If you are having problems sharing already, you can probably resolve those problems by enabling the proper settings as detailed here. With your Windows PC, much of the setup can be accomplished in the Network and Internet window in the Control Panel. You can also enable sharing options directly from a folder.

To enable sharing on your Windows PC (remember, you can only create home groups on Windows 7 and higher):

Tip If you have other Windows 7 (or greater) computers on the network, in order to make sure your PC is set up to share in the best manner possible, configure a home group for them. You can do this from the Network and Sharing Center in Windows 7. If you don't need to create a home group, but you have more than one PC, at least know the name of the workgroup. Common workgroup names are MSHOME and WORKGROUP. You never know when you may need this information when connecting with other computers or your Mac.

1. Click Start, select Control Panel, and then click Choose homegroup and sharing beneath the Network and Internet heading.
2. Select the check boxes next to the libraries you want to share (Documents, Pictures, and so on), as shown in Figure 11-1. If you want to share only one or two specific folders, just select the ones to share.

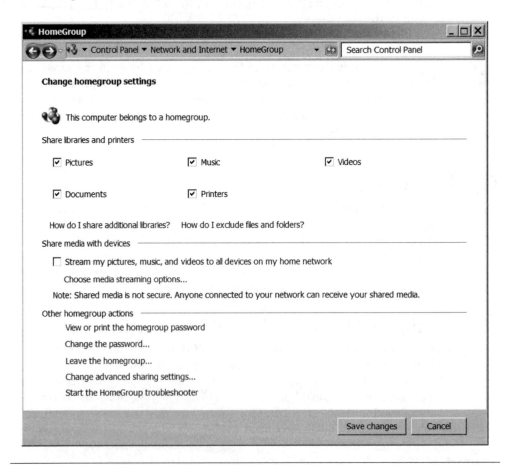

FIGURE 11-1 Enable sharing for libraries and printers from your Windows PC.

3. Click Change advanced sharing settings, and then click the Home or Work heading. A long window with sharing options will display (shown in the next two illustrations).

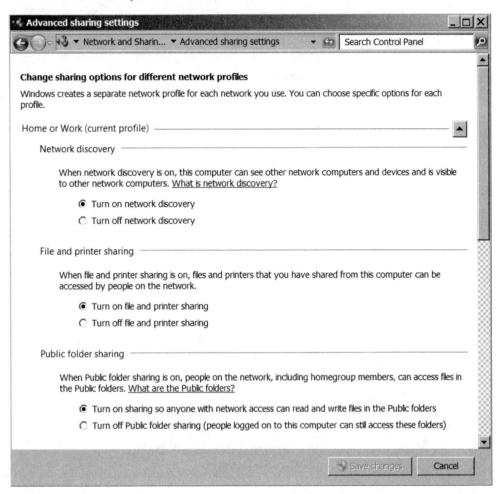

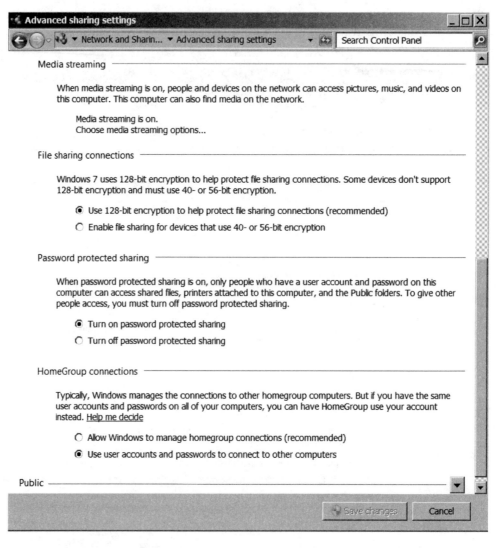

4. Select the radio buttons next to the following options:
   - Turn on network discovery
   - Turn on file and printer sharing
   - Turn on sharing so anyone with network access can read and write files in the Public folders
   - Turn on password protected sharing
   - You can also enable Use user accounts and passwords to connect to other computers if you use both a home group and a workgroup, but the default, to let Windows manage connections, is fine.
5. Click Save changes.

Note You can set up sharing without enabling password protected sharing—but it's not something we recommend. You may choose not to set up passwords if you are the only user on both the PC and the Mac, for example. Otherwise, always require passwords for access to shared resources on your network.

Share a Folder from Your Windows PC

If you want to share just one folder from your Windows computer and do not want to share everything in the Public folder or enable File and Printer Sharing as detailed earlier, you can share that folder manually. You may also opt to share a single folder even if you've enabled sharing and use it regularly. That's because when you enable sharing from a Windows PC, you share specific, predetermined folders. The folder you want to share may not be included in those, and you may not be inclined to move it there. For instance, you may want to share the Taxes folder you keep on your Desktop with your spouse, but not with your four children.

On your Windows 7 PC:

1. Navigate to the folder you want to share.
2. Right-click the folder and select Share with, and then select Specific People. A file-sharing window appears, as shown in Figure 11-2. Select Everyone if you want to share the folder across the network. Otherwise, select a name from the list or click Add to create a new user.

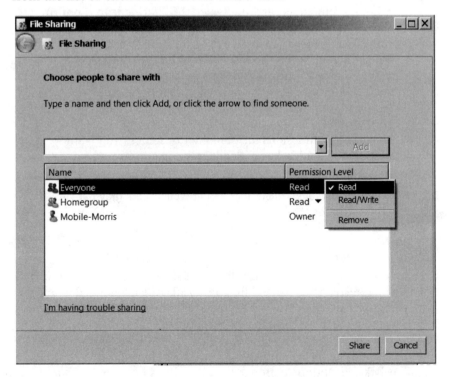

FIGURE 11-2   Share a folder on the network and specify who may access it.

Sharing a folder on a Windows 8 computer is the same as sharing here. In fact, sharing a folder hasn't changed much over the years, except for a new sharing window and the addition of home groups.

3. Set the permissions you want to allow for the folder from the pop-up menu.
4. Click Share to share the selected folder.
5. Click Done to close the File Sharing window.

The safest option is to select Read permissions for most users on your network; that is, if you share at all.

Configure File Sharing from Your Mac

You can share your Mac's files, printers, and optical drive with your PC in much the same way you would share with other Macs, including setting the levels of permissions you want to grant network users. For file sharing, any files you've placed in the Public folders will be shared by default with Read only permission to all network users.

To configure file sharing for your Mac:

1. Open System Preferences from the Dock or click the Apple menu and select System Preferences, and then click the Sharing icon. Confirm that you have file sharing turned on (the status light will be green). You may be prompted to unlock the window and enter the admin password.
2. Select the check box next to File Sharing (see Figure 11-3). File sharing allows you to share any file or folder on your Mac as well as your Public folder.
3. Add a folder you want to share by clicking the plus (+) symbol and finding the folder on your Mac. Select the folder and click Add. To remove a shared folder, select it and click the minus (–) symbol.
4. Select the permissions for the folder or folders you want to share. In most cases, you should choose Read Only.

Once you enable a folder for sharing, you'll see a gray bar with the words "Shared Folder" across the top of the Finder window when you open the folder.

To share files with a Windows PC, you need to enable SMB file sharing. Server Message Block (SMB) is the file sharing protocol used by Windows PCs to share common resources like files, printers, and so on. Macs have their own file sharing protocol, referred to as Apple Filing Protocol (AFP). You need to enable SMB sharing so your Mac can "speak" to your Windows PC and share files and other services.

To enable SMB and select user accounts to share:

1. Open Systems Preferences and click the Sharing icon.
2. Click the Options button. Select the check box next to Share files and folders using SMB (Windows).

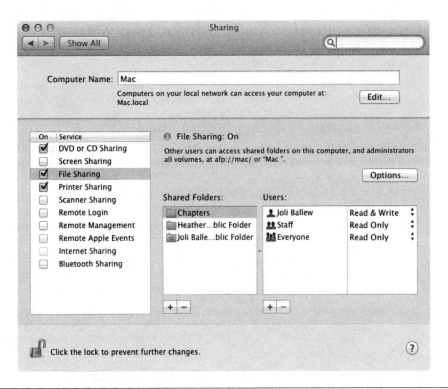

FIGURE 11-3 Configure file sharing and other options in the Sharing window of System Preferences.

3. Choose the user account whose files you want to share by selecting the check box next to the account name (see Figure 11-4). Type the password for the user account when prompted, and then click OK. Click Done when you're finished.

FIGURE 11-4 Choose which user accounts to share.

Configure Printer Sharing from Your Mac

If you want to share your Mac's printer with your Windows PC, you can do this over your network.

To enable printer sharing:

1. Open System Preferences and click the Sharing icon.
2. Select the check box next to Printer Sharing.
3. Select the Printer you want to share (if you have more than one), and then select Everyone in the Users list if you want to allow everyone on the network to use your Mac's printer (see Figure 11-5). Alternatively, you can select one user at a time and select either Can Print or No Access from the pop-up menu to share or limit access to the printer.
4. To add another user for printer sharing, click the plus (+) symbol beneath Users, and then select the user and click the Select button.
5. Close System Preferences.

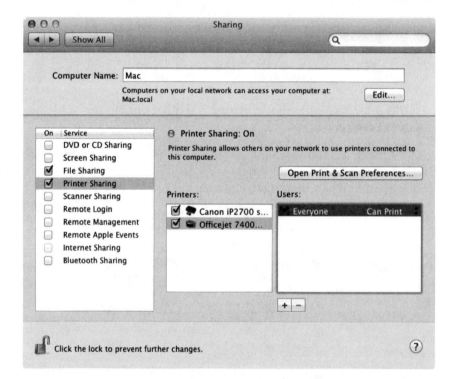

FIGURE 11-5 Share your Mac's printer with others on the network—including a Windows PC user.

To connect your Windows PC to the Mac's printer:

1. Click Start and select Devices and Printers.
2. Click the Add a Printer button on the toolbar and the Add Printer Wizard will start. You should see a window with What Type of Printer Do You Want to Install?
3. Once the wizard locates the Mac printer, click it, and then click Next to finish setting up the printer with the Add Printer Wizard in Windows.

Share Your Mac's Optical Drive

If your Windows PC or even another Mac in your home or office doesn't come with a DVD or CD drive, you can allow others on the network to use the one on your Mac. In effect, your Windows PC users can stream DVD or CD content directly to their computer.

To share your Mac's optical drive:

1. Open System Preferences and click the Sharing icon.
2. Select the check box next to DVD or CD sharing.
3. Select the check box next to Ask me before allowing others to use my DVD drive. This ensures that you'll be aware of when others use the drive and they'll have to wait until you grant permission to access the drive.
4. Close System Preferences.

The Windows PC user can access the DVD or CD drive the same way they would a shared file. The drive, and any video or music content in it, will appear in their shared window when they access the Mac from their computer.

Access Shared Folders from a PC

You can access shared folders from your Windows PC with a user account and password from one of your Mac accounts—including a sharing only account if you set one up. You have to have a working network, though, and the PC must be connected to it, as must the Mac(s). If you need to, connect your computer(s) to the same network.

Before you get started, confirm that your computers are currently connected to the same network—whether Ethernet or wireless. Click Start, and then Select Computer. Under Network, you should see the name of your Mac.

 On a Windows PC, next to the *parent* folders (like Network, Documents, Homegroup and the like) available from the left pane of any Explorer window is a small triangle. You'll have to hover your mouse over a folder for this triangle to appear. If the triangle is facing right, the folder is not "expanded." You can click this triangle to expand the folder (the triangle will then face downward), to show what's in it.

If you are on an Ethernet network and don't see your Mac, check the connections between your Windows PC and the network switch or Ethernet port.

Connect Your PC to a Hidden or Closed Network

If you reconfigured your wireless router to hide the network name (SSID), you'll need to manually set up your Windows PC to connect to the network.

To manually join your wireless network:

1. Click Start and type **Network**, and then click Network and Sharing Center from the menu.
2. Click Connect to a Network, and then click Set Up a Connection or Network.
3. Select Manually connect to a wireless network, and then click Next.
4. Enter the network name, and then select the Security and Encryption types from the drop-down menus.

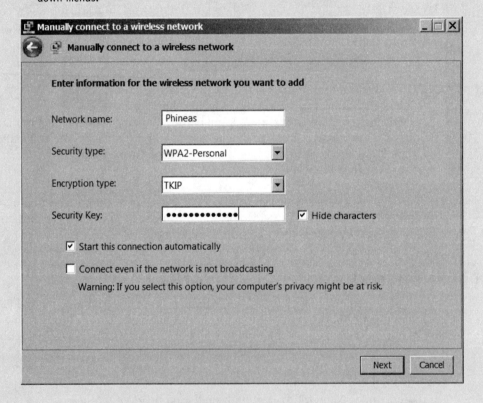

5. Click Next to join the network.

With sharing enabled and a working network, and all of the sharing computers connected and turned on, you are ready to access the shared folders from your PC.

To access shared folders from your Windows PC:

1. Click Start and select Computer.
2. Click the computer name under Network (MacBook, Mac, and so on).

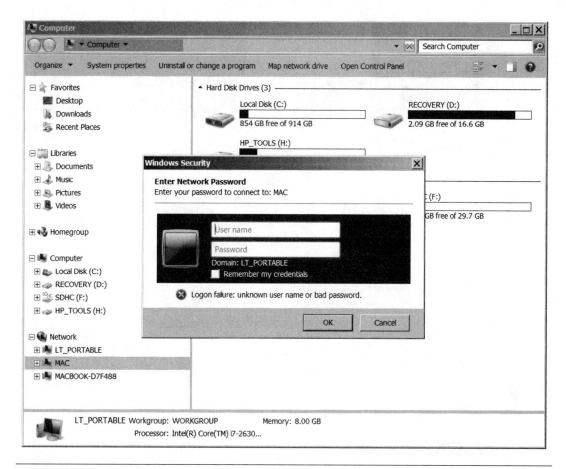

FIGURE 11-6   Enter a Mac user account name and password to access files on your Mac.

3. Enter the user account name and password of the Mac account you want to access (see Figure 11-6).
4. Select Remember my credentials if you want the PC to store the user account and password.

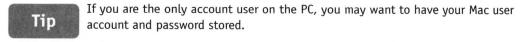

Tip   If you are the only account user on the PC, you may want to have your Mac user account and password stored.

After you enter the name and password, the folders you selected for sharing will appear in the window as shown here. Double-click the shared file to view its contents.

Depending on the permissions that have been set, you may be able to open and view the files and make copies to the folders on your PC.

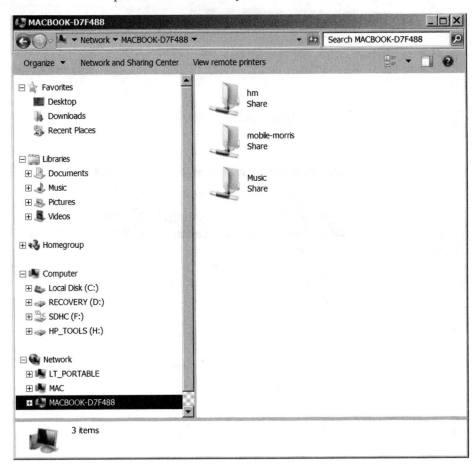

Access Shared Files from Your Mac

There are a few different ways of accessing shared files from your Mac; we'll show you how by using the sidebar in your Finder as well as the Connect to Server option. We'll assume the network is healthy, all computers are turned on, and everyone is connected to the same network.

Access Shared Files in Finder

Connecting to your PC files via your Finder is the most straightforward method for accessing shared files, but it can take a few minutes for your computers to connect and for the shared files to display. You can also access files with the Connect to Server option (we explain next), which can be a faster connection but requires slightly more to set up. If you want to verify that your Mac can "see" the Windows PC, you may need to show the Shared section in your sidebar.

To show your Windows PC in the Finder's sidebar:

1. Select Preferences from the Finder menu, and then click the Sidebar tab.
2. Select the check box next to Connected servers under Shared, and then close the Finder Preferences window.
3. Open a Finder window and check that your Windows PC is displayed under Shared in the sidebar. You may need to click Shared and then select Show from the pop-up.

To connect to the shared files on your Windows PC:

1. Click the name of your PC in the sidebar. An authorization window prompting you to enter the PC user account name and password should display.
2. Click Connect As if you don't see the authorization window appear and wait while it does.
3. Enter the PC user account name and password (see Figure 11-7). Select the check box next to Remember this password in my keychain if you wish.
4. Click Connect.

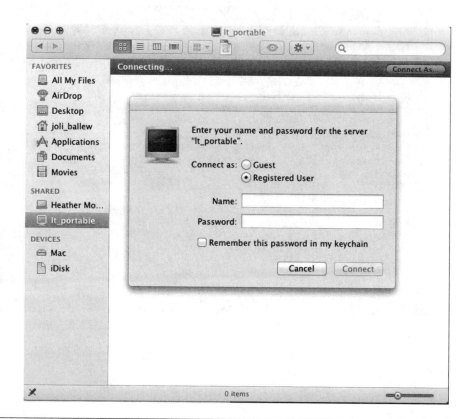

FIGURE 11-7   Connect to a user account on your Windows PC to access shared files.

> **Tip**
>
> If your Mac is protected by a password and only you can access it, and if you log off or lock your computer when you aren't using it, it's okay to let your Mac remember the required passwords to log on to your other computers. If you share a computer with others and have not followed our advice to create a user account for each one, then don't let your Mac remember the passwords.

You will stay connected until you log out of your user account or shut down. If you want to disconnect from the shared folder, you can click the Eject icon next to the folder in the sidebar.

Another way to access shared files from your Mac is to use the Go/Connect to Server option. In order to do this, you'll need the IP address of your Windows PC.

To find your Windows PC's IP address:

1. Click Start and type **cmd** in the search field, and then select cmd from the menu.
2. In the command window, next to the prompt, type **ipconfig**.
3. Look for the address next to IPv4 Address. It will consist of a series of numbers separated by periods.

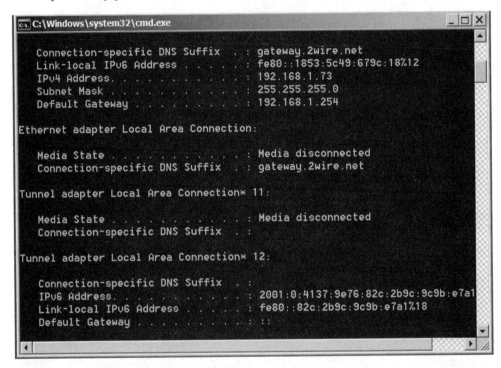

```
C:\Windows\system32\cmd.exe

        Connection-specific DNS Suffix  . : gateway.2wire.net
        Link-local IPv6 Address . . . . . : fe80::1853:5c49:679c:18%12
        IPv4 Address. . . . . . . . . . . : 192.168.1.73
        Subnet Mask . . . . . . . . . . . : 255.255.255.0
        Default Gateway . . . . . . . . . : 192.168.1.254

Ethernet adapter Local Area Connection:

        Media State . . . . . . . . . . . : Media disconnected
        Connection-specific DNS Suffix  . : gateway.2wire.net

Tunnel adapter Local Area Connection* 11:

        Media State . . . . . . . . . . . : Media disconnected
        Connection-specific DNS Suffix  . :

Tunnel adapter Local Area Connection* 12:

        Connection-specific DNS Suffix  . :
        IPv6 Address. . . . . . . . . . . : 2001:0:4137:9e76:82c:2b9c:9c9b:e7a1
        Link-local IPv6 Address . . . . . : fe80::82c:2b9c:9c9b:e7a1%18
        Default Gateway . . . . . . . . . : ::
```

4. Write down the IP address of your Windows PC. This is the address you'll need to use the Go/Connect to Server option from your Mac.

To access your Windows PC's files from your Mac:

1. Click Go from the Finder menu and select Connect to Server or press COMMAND-K.
2. Type **smb://** and your Windows PC's IP address, and then click Connect.

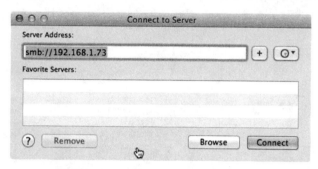

3. Type in the user account name and password of the PC user account you want to access.
4. Select the volume and then click OK.

When you are finished with these steps, you should see the Windows PC under Shared in your Sidebar. Click the computer's IP address in the sidebar and all the shared files on your Windows PC will display. You can open, copy, or save them to your Mac as you would any other file.

Set Login Options to Automatically Connect to Shared Resources

Rather than reconnecting to your PC's folders or shared drives each time you log in to your account, you can make them available to you at login. This is certainly safe provided your Mac is protected by a password that no one knows, and that you log out of your Mac user account when you are not using it.

1. Follow the steps described in the previous section to connect to the shared folder.
2. Click System Preferences in the Dock or click the Apple menu and select System Preferences.
3. Click Users & Groups, and then click the Login Items tab at the top of the window.

4. Drag the shared folder on your desktop to the list box labeled These Items Will Open Automatically When You Log In. If your shared folder is not on the desktop, drag it from a Finder window or click the add (+) button beneath the window and navigate to the folder to add it.

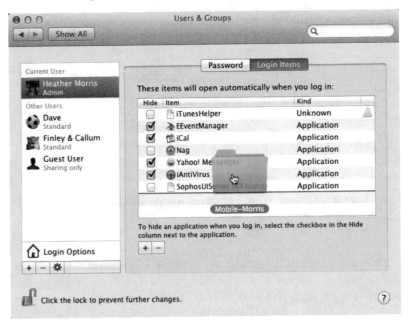

5. Close System Preferences.

Adding Additional Computers to the Network, Including Windows 8

You'll likely continue to add computers to your network. As time passes, computers will fail and you'll replace them with new ones; you'll purchase your first laptop, you'll upgrade the operating systems on the computers you own, and you may even purchase a new Mac. We bet you're pretty confident you can easily add that new Mac. You may feel a twinge of angst if you want to add a Windows 8 machine, though. Have no fear; that Windows 8 machine will be easy to add.

What you'll notice as time goes on is that the newer the operating system, the easier it is to use and configure. This is true of both Macs and PCs. Sure, it may *seem* as though the new OS is completely different, and yes, there may be a learning curve. However, as in the case with Windows 8, you'll still be able to create home groups, you'll still have access to the Network and Sharing Center, you can still right-click a folder to share it and configure sharing options, and you can still put data in the Public folders. Windows 8 still offers the familiar Control Panel (even though you'll configure the less technical aspects in PC Settings); you'll still have access to advanced sharing settings, and so on. So relax and enjoy your network; if you want to add something to it later, it'll be even easier than what you've experienced up to now!

12 Speed Up Booting and Increase Performance

If you've noticed your Mac takes longer to start up and has slowed down a good deal, there are several steps you can take to revive your computer and restore its speed and efficiency. In this chapter we'll look at a number of small changes you can make that, when added together, can speed up the boot process and overall performance of your Mac. We'll also explore how you can monitor the applications and other processes on your computer to keep an eye out for what might be slowing you down.

Review and Limit Login Items

Many applications are set to launch when you first log in to your account or restart your Mac. Having too many login items can increase the time your Mac takes to log you in to your account or restart. Also, it doesn't make any sense to have your Mac launch applications that you don't regularly use. Check which apps are launched at login, and speed up your Mac by reducing their number. You may have added login items yourself, but some applications add login items to your Mac when you first install them, and you may be unaware they were added.

To review and limit which applications start at login:

1. Open System Preferences and click Users & Groups, and then click Login Items.

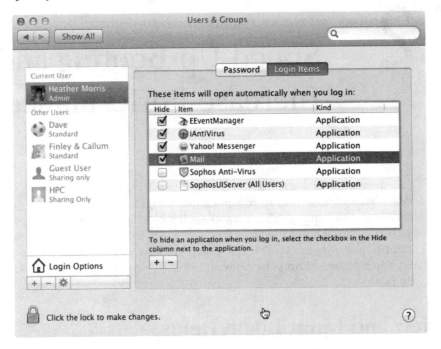

2. Look for items on the list that you don't want to launch at login.
3. Select an item in the list, and then click the (–) minus button to remove it from the login list.

Rather than removing a number of items all at once, start with a few you don't need, and then check for any speed differences at login. If you don't notice a difference, you can repeat the preceding steps with an additional application to further reduce login time.

Note   If you have a favorite application that you don't see in the login items but that you want to include, drag it into the login list or click the plus (+) symbol and find it on your computer. You'll still be waiting at login, but at least when you come back with your cup of coffee, your favorite application will be open and waiting for you.

Close Idle Applications

If your Mac slows down noticeably while you're working throughout the day, check how many applications you have open. Even if all the windows associated with the application are closed, the programs may still be running in the background.

One quick way to get some speed back is to close applications you're not using. Look for the small blue light beneath the applications in the Dock, and don't forget to close Finder windows as well.

Tip There are a number of wonderfully fascinating and fun desktop backgrounds that you can download from the App Store, like 3D Earth and various aquarium backgrounds. Unfortunately, many of these programs eat up a lot of CPU (central processing unit; your computer's processing power) and RAM (random access memory; your computer's memory) and noticeably slow your computer down or worse. Some contain poorly written code that can cause your Mac to freeze up or crash. Limit these backgrounds if your Mac is slowing down, or ditch them altogether if you think they are causing problems.

Explore Logon and Logoff Options

If you use Fast User Switching and leave two accounts logged in at the same time, the user account you are in will slow down. The reason for the drag is that the other user account takes up a portion of your Mac's RAM. If that account has a number of documents and applications open, this will further bog you down. While Fast User Switching is convenient, log out of other accounts if you notice it's taking a long time to perform routine tasks.

To log out of other accounts:

1. Select the user name from the Fast User Switching menu. A logged-in user account will have an orange check next to the name.
2. Have the other account user enter the password, and then click Log In.
3. Select Log out (user name) from the Apple menu, and then click Log Out.

If you are the only person who uses your Mac, you can set it up to log you in automatically. This can shave some time off the startup process. Of course, enabling automatic login also puts your Mac at risk if someone does switch it on without your permission or while you are away from it. An unauthorized user will have instant access to all the information on your computer, including your personal and financial information.

Run Performance Tests

There are a number of ways you can test the performance of your Mac by measuring things like CPU and RAM usage. Your Mac comes with a utility that gives you information about your Mac's performance in these essential areas. There are also free and paid third-party applications, called benchmarking tools, which give you an overall score of your computer's performance and can be helpful when trying to figure out how to improve your Mac's performance.

Run Activity Monitor

Activity Monitor is a built-in utility that comes with OS X and provides you with information about your Mac's performance in real time. Activity Monitor displays how much RAM is currently in use and also displays information about how much disk space is available, and CPU usage, as well as details about your network's performance. This information can give you clues about processes that are taking up your computer's resources, and which of those you can potentially limit to improve your Mac's performance. Processes refer to activities like your Notification Center or anti-virus program that you won't see running, but there are also many processes related to all the computations OS X performs to keep your Mac running. Of course, processes also refer to applications that you can see, like Safari or Finder.

To assess CPU usage in Activity Monitor:

1. Click Launchpad and click Other, then Activity Monitor.
2. Click the CPU tab. You'll see a list of active processes, which is updated every few seconds (see Figure 12-1). At the bottom of the window is a summary of how the CPU is being shared between the user (you) and the system, and what percentage of CPU is idle.

Click the % CPU column header to sort the list from highest to lowest. When the arrow icon in the header is pointing down, the applications or processes at the top are

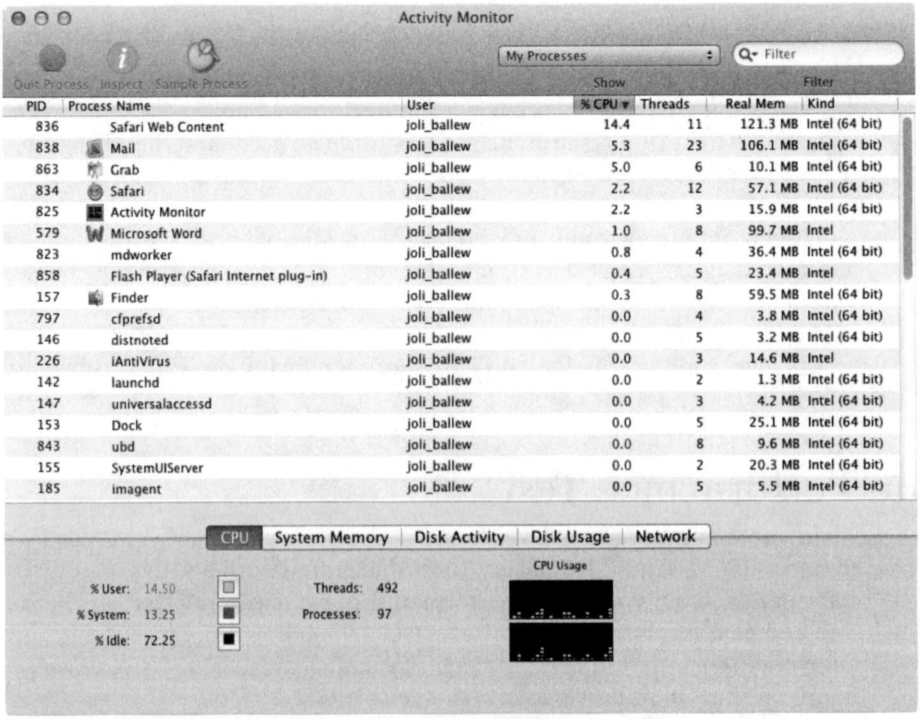

FIGURE 12-1 CPU usage as shown in Activity Monitor

the ones that are taking up the greatest amount of CPU. If you notice one process or application is taking up a lot of CPU power, try quitting it from within the application to see if that has an effect on your Mac's performance. You can watch for a change in Activity Monitor. If the application doesn't quit, you can click Quit Process in Activity Monitor, and then click Quit. You should also look out for any background application in the list that you downloaded but no longer use. If one of these appears to be eating up CPU power, quit it or consider uninstalling it completely from your Mac.

Caution If you selected All Processes from the pop-up menu at the top of Activity Monitor, essential system processes will display that you shouldn't stop or interfere with. If you see a process owned by root, leave it alone as stopping it could disable your computer.

To monitor RAM usage:

1. Click Launchpad in the Dock and click Other.
2. Click Activity Monitor and check that the System Memory tab is selected. The breakdown of RAM usage is by the following four types of RAM:
   - **Free** The amount of RAM currently available for use.
   - **Wired** Memory that is currently being used by OS X for essential computing tasks and not available.
   - **Active** Memory that is in use now by applications you are running.
   - **Inactive** RAM that's been used recently by an application but isn't free yet.

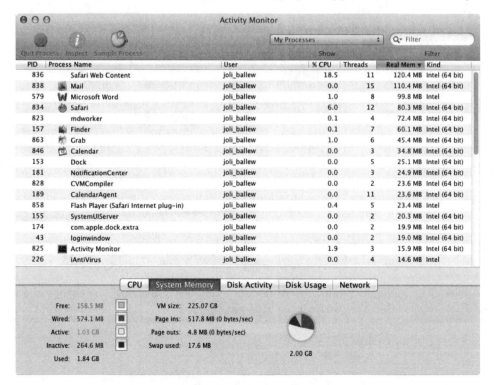

You can monitor which applications are taking up the most RAM in Activity Monitor by clicking the Real Mem column. If you notice one application is taking up a huge amount of memory, quit it from within the application and watch for a change in Free RAM in Activity Monitor. If you can't quit it normally, select the application from the list in Activity Monitor and click Quit Process, and then click Quit.

You can also keep track of RAM over several days to see how much RAM you have free on any given day while running applications you need. If the colored chart is mostly green and blue, then the amount of RAM you currently have is probably fine. However, if you notice that the chart consists of mostly red and yellow and that the Wired and Active RAM is using up most of the RAM, you may be running low. If you only check Activity Monitor once, you can get a false impression that you are low on Free RAM. OS X holds a portion of RAM in Inactive RAM right after you close an application. It retains it in case you reopen the application again (a fairly common computing scenario). Holding it in this way makes it easier to launch the application the second time. However, as you watch RAM in Activity Monitor over time, you should see more than 10 percent free RAM when working with several of your favorite applications and documents.

The best way to deal with consistently low RAM is to add more but, if you can't, closing applications that are RAM hogs is one quick way to improve your Mac's performance.

Tip See "Add RAM If Your Mac Is Short" in Chapter 1 for information on how to add RAM and instantly improve your Mac's performance.

Consider Using Third-Party Benchmarking Tools

Benchmarking tools test your Mac's performance in a number of areas and assign a score when the test is complete. The score on its own isn't terrifically useful, although you can compare your Mac's score with others online. This information comes in handy before and after you make changes to improve your Mac's performance. For example, after you follow some of the suggestions in this book (like updating software, deleting unwanted or unnecessary applications, or upgrading your RAM), then you might perform another benchmarking test to assess whether these things have improved your Mac's performance.

There are a few benchmarking tools you can use for free, including NovaBench (free in the App Store), which tests RAM and CPU speeds, and also performs graphics and hardware tests. Another well-known tool is Geekbench, which has a free version online at www.primatelabs.ca/geekbench as well as a paid version in the App Store. Geekbench only tests the performance of your Mac's CPU and RAM.

Tip If you do decide to run a benchmarking test, make only one change at a time to see whether what you've done has improved your Mac's performance. If you run a test after making several changes, you won't know which of the changes made the difference.

Running a benchmarking program is fairly quick and easy to do; you just have to set aside some time to do it and decide what you want to get out of it. You should run an initial test to get the baseline scores and then another test after you've made changes. To run NovaBench, open the program from Launchpad and click Run Benchmarks, as shown in Figure 12-2.

Keep in mind that if you run NovaBench with other applications open, it will affect your score. You can close all your other applications if you want to see how fast your Mac is compared to other similar models. However, running it while your most frequently used applications are open will give you information about how your Mac performs under normal use. When the test is complete, you'll get scores for your computer, as shown in Figure 12-3.

The four scores you get after the first test (RAM, CPU, Graphics and Hardware) are the ones that you should use to measure your Mac's results over time or after you make changes. A higher score is better, so you should see the numbers go up after you make performance changes to your Mac or when you have fewer applications open while running the test. If you want to compare your Mac's scores with other computers, click Submit and Compare in the results window. You'll go to the NovaBench web site where you can register and submit the scores for your performance test and compare results with similar Mac models.

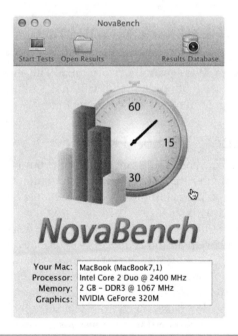

FIGURE 12-2   Run benchmarking tests with NovaBench.

FIGURE 12-3 Results from a NovaBench test

Enhance Hard Disk Performance

You can make a number of small changes to your Mac that, added together, can have an impact on your Mac's overall performance. The suggestions we make in this next section are not fixes that on their own will make a huge difference, but when added together, they can revive your sluggish machine.

Get the Latest Device Drivers

Device drivers are a type of software that allows your Mac to interact with hardware and serves as a sort of interpreter between your computer and devices like scanners, printers, and other common types of hardware. While Apple Software Update automatically installs updated drivers for Apple hardware, you have to manually update drivers for most non-Apple hardware. You should keep your drivers up to date for the same reasons you keep your other applications updated—to take advantage of improvements and bug fixes that keep your Mac healthy and performing the way you want.

If you aren't notified that there is an update to your drivers, you can go to the manufacturer's web site and look for updates. Search for your hardware type on the site or look for the downloads section. If you see a more recent version than the one you have, consider downloading it (unless it's a beta driver, in which case you should avoid downloading it until a final driver is released).

Change Your Display Settings

Some applications will run better if you change the display settings. If you aren't getting the display quality you want in a graphics or video game, look in the Read Me files for the application to locate the recommended display setting for the application. Often, a lower display setting can enhance the performance of the application. When you locate the correct display settings, do the following:

1. Open System Preferences and click Displays.
2. Select the Scaled option button and then choose the resolution.

Explore Network Storage

Buying and installing a Network Attached Storage (NAS) device is one way to free up space on your hard disk and make sharing files with others on your network easier and safer. Whether you have an all-Mac network in your home or one composed of a combination of Macs and Windows computers, you can find an NAS device that all computers can access and use. Having an NAS device is like having your own small file server in your home. They vary in size from 500GB to 2TB and prices range from $100 and up. Most devices connect directly to your router via Ethernet. Some of the potential benefits and drawbacks of NAS storage are outlined next.

Benefits:

- Save space on your hard disk and keep your Mac healthy.
- Share files with others on the network without having to grant access to the home folder on your Mac and configure permissions.
- Share large media files like music, video, and photos.

Drawbacks:

- Many NAS devices don't work with Time Machine but often come with their own software to support regular backups.
- Backups have to be performed from each computer separately with a backup program you choose or one that comes with your NAS device.
- Your Mac's performance will be worse with an NAS device attached.

You can set up an NAS device fairly quickly through the setup wizard software that is included with it. You can configure individual accounts for each person to access the device and set up a Public folder that everyone can use to share files (for example, music, video, and images). You should keep all of your personal files, including those in your home folder, on your Mac rather than on an NAS device.

Replace Buggy Applications

If you have a problematic application that is either constantly slowing you down or crashing frequently and unexpectedly, it's possible that it has a bug and needs to be replaced. Of course, there are a number of other reasons that applications misbehave, including a shortage of RAM or a damaged file. However, if you find that slowdowns and crashes only happen with a particular application, it's probably a good candidate for replacement.

However, before replacing it completely, check whether there are any updates in the App Store or on the developer's web site. If an update is available, download it and check whether there are any improvements to its behavior. You should also check to see if damaged preference files are the source of the problem. See the "Problematic Preference Files" sidebar in Chapter 2.

If you are convinced you have a dud on your hands, open Applications and use the uninstaller if it has one. If it doesn't, drag the application icon in question into the Trash, and then select Empty Trash from the Finder menu.

When you look for a replacement for your wayward application, focus your search in the App Store rather than on third-party web sites. Bugs are more common among applications developed by small third-party developers who may submit their apps to fewer or less rigorous tests (or none at all!). While applications from the App Store are by no means immune to bugs, you at least have the reassurance of many reviews and some security in the knowledge that the developers are part of Apple's developers' network.

Make Use of Power Nap

You can boost the performance of your Mac and conserve energy by enabling the Power Nap feature that was included with Mountain Lion OS X. While your Mac sleeps, Power Nap checks for software updates, new email and messages, backs up to Time Machine—and more. The activities it performs depend on the setting you enable, as we'll explain.

The only downside to Power Nap is that it isn't compatible with all Mac models. Only the following models can currently use Power Nap: Mid 2012 MacBook Pro with Retina Display and the Mid 2011 and Mid 2012 MacBook Air models. To support Power Nap, you need to download an SMC firmware update, which you can find on Apple's support page, http://support.apple.com/kb/HT5394.

There are two power options for using Power Nap: one that is enabled while your Mac is connected to a power adapter and one that you can use while it's using battery power. The former is enabled by default. You can opt to use just one or both.

To enable Power Nap on your compatible Mac (and after you update the SMC firmware), launch System Preferences from the Dock and click Energy Saver. In the Power Adapter tab, you'll notice that Enable power nap while plugged into a power adapter is enabled by default. There is also another option you can enable under the Battery tab. To use Power Nap while on battery power, select the check box next to Enable power nap while on battery power.

Note If you enable the battery power option and your Mac is low on battery power, Power Nap will stop performing its behind-the-scene checks until your computer is connected to a power adapter again.

The tasks Power Nap performs depends on which option you enabled. With the battery power option enabled, Power Nap:

- Receives new Mail messages.
- Updates Calendar.
- Updates Reminders with any changes you make on your iOS device or additional Mac.
- Updates Photo Stream with new photos you've added.

With the power adapter option enabled (and with your Mac connected to a power source), Power Nap can perform the following additional tasks:

- Checks for updates to Apple software and downloads them (but doesn't install them)
- Performs Time Machine backups
- Updates Help Center as available

The benefit of all this activity is that when you wake your Mac from sleep, many of the processes it usually performs on waking will already be running. You can get straight to work and you won't be slowed down waiting for software updates or other tasks your Mac usually performs when it wakes up.

13 Improve Security

Following good security practices is central to keeping your Mac healthy, and hopefully you have already followed some of the suggestions in previous chapters, like creating separate user accounts for everyone who uses the Mac, enabling the firewall, and protecting yourself against data loss by backing up your Mac regularly. In this chapter, we'll look at additional measures you can take to improve the security of your Mac and your personal information, including physically securing your Mac, making use of the keychain, changing your passwords regularly, and more.

Enhance Physical Security

While there are countless software tools you can employ to keep your Mac safe, it's worth considering what you can do to keep your computer physically secure. Macs have always been attractive targets for theft, and computers like MacBooks and MacMinis that are compact and easily portable are especially attractive to would-be thieves. To begin with, simple common sense measures can improve security, like not advertising your computer's existence by placing it next to a large window, or buying a carrying case with a lock when you are on the go with a laptop. We'll look at some other options next.

To keep your Mac safe in your home or office, you can physically secure it by using the built-in security slot that is included on many models (as well as other hardware such as monitors, external hard drives, and AirPort base stations). The security slot is a tiny, elongated oval-shaped hole on the side of your Mac or in the back, depending on your model. The slot, called the Kensington Security slot after the company that patented it, accepts a specially designed security lock attached to a cable that you then tether to a desk or some other sturdy object. Once the lock is inserted, you have some protection against a thief walking away with your computer. The lock also offers some modest protection against someone opening the case and interfering with or removing things like your RAM, hard drive, and other internal components. However, a really determined thief could get through the cables with a wire or bolt cutter. The locks and cables can be purchased in the Apple store and at other computer store retailers.

Tip   If you are sending a young person and their Mac laptop off to a university of their choice, consider purchasing one of these locks and cables as a deterrent to campus thieves.

If your Mac doesn't have a security slot and you don't plan to move it from its present location, there are brackets and enclosures you can buy to mount your computer to your desk. Another simple option for a laptop is to invest in a laptop locker, which you can place your MacBook in when you're not using it.

Note   If your Mac has been lost or stolen, you can use Find My Mac in iCloud to locate it on a map. You have to enable this on your computer before using it (not after your Mac is lost). For information on how to set this up, see "View Your iCloud Account and Try the Find My ... Function" in Chapter 8.

Apply Advanced Security Settings

In the Security & Privacy window of System Preferences, you have additional options for protecting your Mac and important data contained on it. You can configure your Mac to log out automatically after a period of inactivity that you set. If you step away for a minute and don't log out of your Mac, you put your computer at risk of interference if someone uses it while you are still logged in. This is especially true if you work in a very busy environment or have young children in the home who may sit down and "play" on the computer if you step away.

Another security setting that you might want to enable is requiring an administrator password to access locked preferences. This includes all the many preferences you've set up to keep your Mac safe, like user account passwords, Sharing preferences, and any security items you've enabled. If someone can access your user account after you step away, they can get into these preferences and make changes that could compromise the security and health of your Mac.

To enable both of these security options:

1. Click System Preferences in the Dock and click Security & Privacy.
2. Click the Advanced button.
3. Select the check box next to Require an administrator password to access locked preferences.

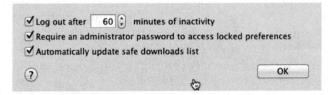

4. To automatically log out of your user account after a set period of inactivity, select the check box next to Log out after ... and then select a number of minutes by typing into the field or clicking up or down on the arrows.
5. Click OK when you are done.

In the same window, you'll also see "Automatically update safe downloads list." This setting is enabled by default, so that your Mac updates the list of safe downloads that Apple keeps. The list includes applications that Apple has confirmed are free from known malware that you might download while in Safari or Mail. If the check box next to this option isn't enabled, select it now to keep your Mac safe.

Work with OS X Keychain

Keychain is a built-in utility that remembers user names and passwords you access regularly, and stores them in an encrypted format. Rather than having to remember a dozen individual passwords, you only need to remember one. This is useful when you create longer, more complex (and thus more secure) passwords for things like your wireless network and web site or application passwords. You've probably made use of the keychain without even being aware of it. When you enter a password for a server, for example, you will see the window shown in Figure 13-1. If you selected the "Remember this password in my keychain" check box, then the password will be stored and you won't have to remember it each time you want to connect.

Your keychain is unlocked automatically each time you log in to your user account, providing you with easy access to all the passwords you saved. The downside of this is that anyone who happens across your computer while you are still logged in (and provided you haven't locked it) can potentially access all the resources that you have password protected. In this next section, we'll show you how to secure your keychain and manage the passwords you have saved there.

Change Your Keychain Password

To keep your keychain—and all your saved user names and passwords—secure, consider changing your keychain password to prevent anyone from accessing its contents after you log in. Your keychain shares the same password as your user account by default and is unlocked when you log in. Anyone who accesses your Mac when you step away from

> Enter your name and password for the server "macbook".
>
> Connect as: ○ Guest
>   ● Registered User
>
> Name: [   ]
>
> Password: [   ]
>
> ☐ Remember this password in my keychain
>
> [Change Password...]   [Cancel] [Connect]

FIGURE 13-1   A Connect to Server window with the option of saving the password in your keychain

it could conceivably access your keychain and use the passwords to access your accounts on web sites or other resources you'd prefer to keep secure. To improve the security of your passwords, change your keychain password by doing the following:

1. Open Launchpad from the Dock, click Other, and then click Keychain Access.
2. Select your keychain from the list on the left. It will be in bold lettering and either be labeled "login" or your short user name.

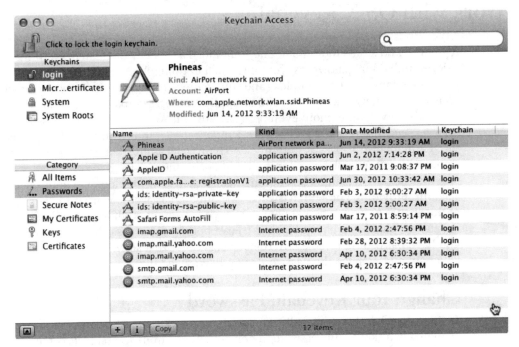

3. Click Edit from the menu and select Change Password for Keychain "login" (or the name of the keychain).
4. Type the existing password in the first field, and then enter the new password in the following two fields and click OK.

After you change your keychain password, you'll notice that the next time you go to use a password, OS X will prompt you to provide the password when an application needs to access the keychain, even if that application had access before.

Use Password Assistant to Help You Create Strong Passwords

Password Assistant is built into OS X and helps you generate stronger and more secure passwords. You may have noticed the small key icon next to the New password field when you changed the keychain password or when you created or changed a password for a user account on your Mac. It's not a program you can open and launch anytime you need some help generating a password; rather, it is available when you are working within OS X applications that require good passwords like Keychain and Users and Groups in System Preferences.

To put Password Assistant to work for you, click the key icon near the New password field you are typing into. It shows you the relative strength of the password you're entering and can even make suggestions for creating stronger ones. You have a few options for creating safe passwords, including manually creating one and getting feedback while you type, or having Password Assistant generate one for you. Often just the addition of a few extra symbols or numbers can improve a password's security.

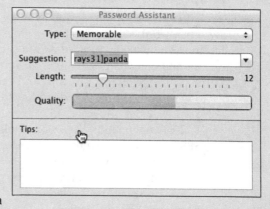

To manually create a password:

1. Click the key symbol next to the New password field.
2. Type your new password in the Suggestion field to test it. While you type, Password Assistant will make suggestions for improving the password like adding number or symbols or increasing its length. The security of the password is shown at the colored bar at the bottom—you want an all-green field. If your password turns the colored bar red or yellow, keep experimenting with combinations.

If you want Password Assistant to generate password suggestions for you, click the pop-up menu next to Type at the top of the window. You can choose from the following:

- **Memorable**   This option creates passwords with phrases, letters, and symbols that are easier to remember.
- **Letters & Numbers**   This creates password combinations from the alphabet and numbers.
- **Numbers Only**   Generates a password based on random numbers.

(*continued*)

- **Random**   Creates very strong passwords with a random combination of characters including letters, numbers, and symbols. The passwords can be hard, if not impossible, to remember without writing them down.
- **FIPS-181 Compliant**   A U.S. government password standard that probably won't apply to most users.

For most users, the Memorable option is the best. It will generate a password that, hopefully, you won't forget easily. If you want to increase the length of the password, click and drag on the slider bar next to Length to create longer, and more secure, passwords.

Manage Your Passwords in Keychain

Keychain saves all the passwords you tell it to—even if they're wrong. If you opt to save a password, say on a web site while in Safari, and type it in incorrectly, keychain will save the mistaken password. You can check the passwords in Keychain Access and edit and delete any you need to. You may also change your passwords from time to time (which we'll recommend) and keep Keychain Access up to date.

To view and edit passwords in Keychain Access:

1. Click Launchpad in the Dock, click Other, and then click Keychain Access.
2. Select the login keychain on the left or the main keychain for your user account.
3. Find a password you want to view or edit and double-click it.
4. Select the check box next to Show password. You will be prompted to select Allow (to show the password once), or Always Allow (the password will always be shown after you select this).

> **Keychain Access wants to use your confidential information stored in "twitter.com (example@mail.com)" in your keychain.**
>
> To allow this, enter the "login" keychain password.
>
> Password: [   ]
>
> (?)   [Always Allow]   [Deny]   [Allow]

5. If one of the passwords is incorrect, or you no longer want it in the keychain, you can delete it from the keychain. Select it in the list and press the DELETE key.

Improve Security in Safari

If you enabled it to do so, Safari saves the passwords and user names for web sites you visit frequently. In addition, the Auto Fill option automatically includes your personal details like home address and telephone number from Contacts to help you fill in web forms. Although Auto Fill is convenient, you should consider disabling these options for web sites that contain sensitive information or if you share your user account with someone else.

Disable AutoFill

To prevent Safari from accessing your personal information from Contacts and filling in web forms for you, do the following:

1. Launch Safari from the Dock and select Preferences from the Safari menu, or press COMMAND-comma.
2. Click the AutoFill tab.
3. Clear the check boxes next to Using info from my Contacts card and User names and passwords.

Remove Saved Passwords

If you enabled Safari to save user names and passwords, you'll see the window prompt shown in Figure 13-2. Once you disable this feature by clearing the check box in Safari

FIGURE 13-2   You can allow Safari to save web site passwords.

Preferences next to User names and passwords, you'll want to remove the passwords Safari has saved up until then.

To remove web site passwords from Safari:

1. Launch Safari from the Dock and select Preferences from the Safari menu, or press COMMAND-comma.
2. Click the Passwords tab. Select the passwords you want to delete or click the Remove All button.

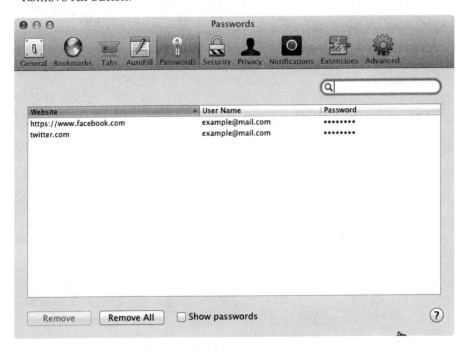

Change Your Passwords to Make Them Stronger

To increase the security of sensitive information on your Mac, your network, and any online account you regularly access, you should change your passwords so that they are "strong." By doing so, you make it harder for hackers and automated hacking software to discover them. A strong password contains upper- and lowercase letters, numbers, and one or two symbols.

Change Your User Account Password

Increase the strength of your user account password to keep your personal information safe and to prevent anyone from interfering with the settings, especially in the administrative account.

To change a user account password:

1. Click System Preferences in the Dock and click Users & Groups.
2. Select your user name and click Change Password.
3. Enter your old password and type in the new, as shown here.

Create a Strong Network Password

If you have a wireless network that users access with a password, it is important to create a strong password to keep your network secure. In addition to the password to join the network, your wireless router may have an administrative password that you should also create a strong password for. See "Change Security Settings on Your Router" in Chapter 10 for information on how to do this.

If you haven't already done so, ensure that you have the most secure encryption type for your wireless network. If you don't have an encryption protocol in place or if you are still using WEP, all of the information that you submit while online can be observed in transit. You should use WPA to keep your wireless network secure. See the instructions on how to check the encryption type in the section "Change Security Settings on Your Router" in Chapter 10.

Set a Firmware Password

Firmware is a combination of software and hardware, such as read-only memory, and Mac OS X includes firmware. Firmware performs a number of functions, but one important feature is its ability to limit the way your Mac can be started. As you may know, you can boot your Mac in a number of different ways like starting up from an external hard drive or from an optical disc. This process is accomplished by holding down specific keys during startup. For example, to select another drive to boot from, you hold down the OPTION key while your Mac is starting up. With Lion and Mountain Lion, you have the option of booting from the Recovery HD (see the following Note). However, as you bypass the normal login process with these methods, anyone else could conceivably boot your Mac without your knowledge and access the contents of your computer or reset any user account password, including the Administrator's password.

Note The Recovery HD is a hidden partition on your hard disk that was created when you upgraded to Lion or Mountain Lion or included on a Mac that came with Mountain Lion. It contains a number of utilities to help you troubleshoot your Mac and accomplish other maintenance tasks. The Recovery HD will be explored more in Chapter 14. For now, it's important to know that you don't want anyone else to be able to boot to your Recovery HD.

If you don't set a Firmware password, someone who accesses your Mac can boot from another disk, drive (or Mac), or boot to the Recovery HD in OS X Recovery and can easily remove your personal files or reset any user account password. To add this extra layer of security to your Mac, do the following:

1. Restart your Mac or press the On button if it's off. When you first hear the startup chimes, press and hold down OPTION-R. Wait while your Mac boots.
2. You should see the OS X Recovery window as shown in Figure 13-3.
3. From the menu at the top, click Utilities and select Firmware Password.
4. Enter a new password in the field, and then click OK.

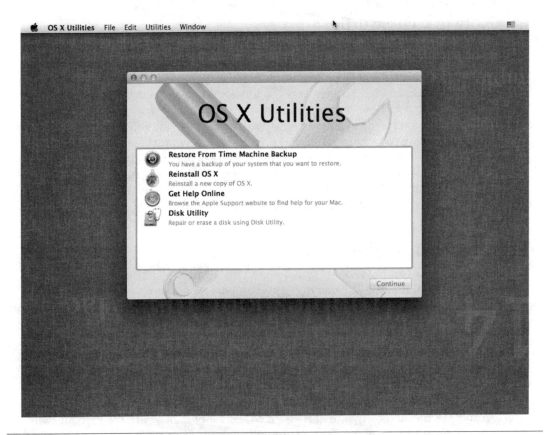

FIGURE 13-3   The OS X Recovery screen in Mountain Lion

14 Troubleshoot Your Mac

All Macs run into problems with buggy applications and slowdowns at some point in time. Whether the problems you encounter are minor glitches or major hard drive issues, you can follow a range of troubleshooting steps, from simple fixes like Force Quitting a badly behaved application to reinstalling OS X in the case of a completely unresponsive or ailing hard drive. We'll look at these steps in this chapter and give you plenty of other tips to help you resolve some of the common problems that can crop up on your Mac.

Simple Fixes

If you have an application that gets hung up or crashes unexpectedly, or if your Mac has slowed down, the solutions to these problems can often be found with just a few simple fixes. Many problems can be resolved by doing things like restarting your Mac or making sure you have the most recent software updates. Before undertaking any major steps to resolve issues with your computer, try the suggestions in this section to restore your Mac to its former pep.

Force Quit an Application

If a program stops responding the way you want or you can't quit, you may need to use the Force Quit option. Click the Apple menu and select Force Quit. From the list, choose the application that you want to exit, as shown here, and click Force Quit. Occasionally, the first attempt at applying Force Quit doesn't work. Repeat these steps to quit the program.

Another option for quitting an unresponsive application is to right-click it in the Dock and then press the OPTION key to reveal the Force Quit command. Select Force Quit from the pop-up menu to exit the app.

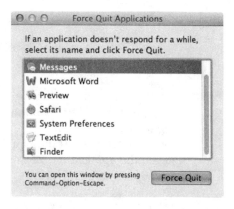

Finally, you can use Activity Monitor to quit a troublesome application. Click Launchpad, click Other, and then open Activity Monitor. In the list that appears, select the application you want to quit and click the red Quit Process icon. Confirm that you want to quit by clicking that button.

If these steps don't work, you can restart your computer by holding down the power button for 10 seconds. When your Mac is off, restart it again by pressing the power button.

Restart Your Mac

Restarting your Mac can often solve a number of problems, especially if it's been left on for a week or more without a shutdown. Temporary files that are created when you work or surf the Web can accumulate and begin to slow you down. When you restart your computer, these file types will be deleted automatically, which will instantly give you back some space and speed.

First, try selecting Restart from the Apple menu to restart your Mac. If that doesn't work (maybe your Mac is frozen or slow to respond), you can use the keyboard shortcut COMMAND-CONTROL and press the EJECT key. Your Mac should restart right away.

Failing all of this, press and hold down the power button for 10 seconds and wait for the power light to go off. When your Mac is off, press the power button again to restart it.

Get Software Updates

If restarting your Mac or Force Quitting an application doesn't seem to solve the problem you're having with your computer, check that you are up to date with the most recent software, whether it's your OS X or any of the applications you regularly use. Many problems and glitches are caused by bugs (in Apple applications or some third-party type you've installed). Bugs are an inevitable part of life, and as a result, the people who create the applications regularly include fixes in updates to sort out any problems.

To check for updates to Apple software and apps you purchased in the App Store:

1. Click the Apple menu and select Software Update.
2. Click the Update button for any applications that have available updates.

Checking for updates for third-party software that you didn't download from the App Store is usually done from within the application. If you're lucky, some applications check for updates each time you open them or download updates for you automatically. If not, you'll need to locate the Check for Updates command within the application. Failing that, you can check for any available updates on the developer's web site.

> **Tip** See the section "Look For and Install Available Updates" in Chapter 1 for more information on how to manage regular Apple software updates.

Log In to a Different User Account

If you set up an emergency user account for troubleshooting, now is the time to use it to help you diagnose whether a problem you are having with an application is specific to your account, or is a problem on your hard drive. If you didn't set up such an account, you might like to do so now by launching System Preferences and clicking Users & Groups. In the Users & Groups window, click the plus (+) symbol beneath Login Options. Enter a new account name and password and click Create User. The new account will be completely free of awkward login items or troublesome preference files, and you may be able to work out problems in your account by comparing the behavior of an application in the two accounts.

Alternatively, you could ask another user if you can log in with their account for troubleshooting purposes.

Log out of your current account by clicking the Apple menu and selecting Log Out. Log in to the emergency account and open the application that crashed in your main user account. If it doesn't crash or otherwise misbehave, you can be fairly sure that the problem resides with your home folder. Often the problems stem from recently added applications and their support files in the Library, or if they were added as a login item.

To identify problem files in your Library:

1. Open Finder and select Macintosh HD from the sidebar.
2. Click the Library Folder and locate and open the Application Support folder.

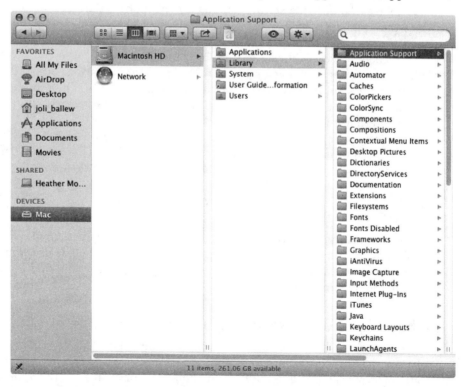

3. Look for recently added items and remove them.

To locate newly added Login items that may be problematic:

1. Open System Preferences from the Dock and click Users & Groups.
2. Click the Login Items tab and look for any items that were added recently.
3. Select the item in the list and then click the minus (–) symbol to remove it.

Tip Preferences files can become damaged and cause applications to crash and cause other problems. See the sidebar "Problematic Preference Files" in Chapter 2 for information on how to troubleshoot problems you're having with an application by deleting selected preference files.

Use Safe Boot

If you can't get your Mac to start up or if it crashes soon after, you can boot to Safe Mode (also called Safe boot) to have your OS X check for problems. When you perform a Safe boot, OS X automatically scans your hard drive and makes repairs to any problems it finds.

To boot in Safe Mode:

1. Press the power button to turn your Mac on (if it's off) or select Restart from the Apple menu.
2. When you hear the startup chimes, press and hold the SHIFT key until you see the Apple logo appear on the screen.

The boot process will take much longer in Safe mode because your OS X is busy behind the scenes checking for problems and performing various other tasks like disabling many third-party items, login items, and fonts. After all of this activity is finished, you'll see your regular login screen with the addition of the words Safe Boot in red lettering at the top.

Log in to your user account and check how things are working. Some features, like file sharing and many third-party applications, will not be available. Once you're satisfied things are working better, restart your Mac to exit Safe Mode.

Check for Errors

A number of common errors that occur on OS X can be diagnosed and sometimes resolved with your Mac's built-in Disk Utility application. You can also troubleshoot errors in cache files and change the default application for certain files to make them open in the program you prefer.

Check for Permission Errors

The permissions that are assigned to your files and folders (the information about who can read, write, and so on) sometimes get muddled and cause problems. This common error can prevent you from opening a file or even an entire application.

Fortunately, there is a troubleshooting process built into OS X to deal with this in Disk Utility.

To check for permission errors:

1. Click Go in the Finder menu and select Utilities.
2. Double-click Disk Utility.
3. Select a disk you want to check permissions on.
4. Click the First Aid tab to display that window (as shown in Figure 14-1).
5. Select the check box next to Show details.
6. Click the Verify Disk Permissions button and wait while Disk Utility verifies the permissions on your selected disk. You will see a time estimate in the lower corner of the Disk Utility window.
7. When the process is complete, you get a message telling you if permissions problems were identified. If none are found, you can close Disk Utility. If the utility identifies any problems, click Repair Disk Permissions (see Figure 14-2) and wait while Disk Utility works.

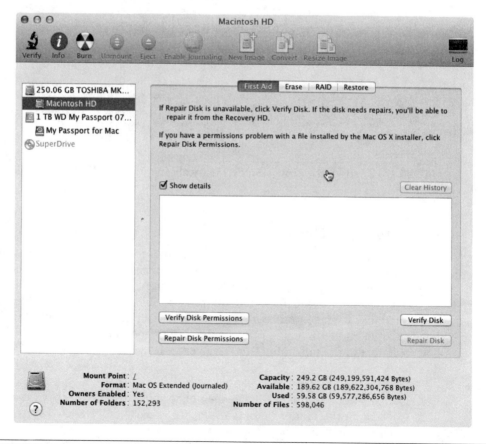

FIGURE 14-1   Disk Utility scans your disk for permission errors.

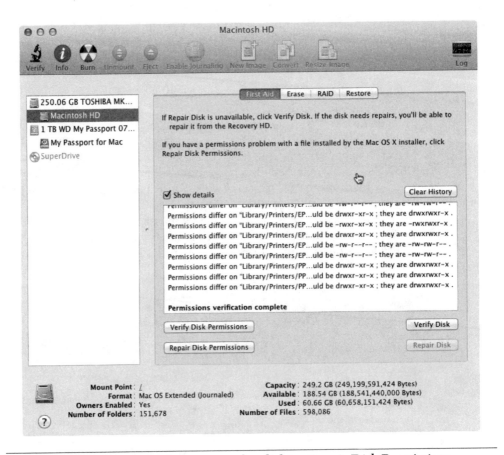

FIGURE 14-2 Repair permission errors by clicking Repair Disk Permissions.

Identify Disk Errors

When they occur, disk errors can cause a range of issues on your Mac, like data loss, or they may even prevent your computer from starting up. When problems start popping up regularly, check your hard disk for errors and repair them. You can look for disk errors with Disk Utility, but you won't be able to fix them there. Repairing an ailing hard disk is made more complicated by the fact that you can't use the disk and repair it at the same time; you'll have to boot from another disk to fix it. We'll explain how to do that in the upcoming "Use Recovery HD" section. First, check if your hard disk contains errors:

1. Quit any applications you have open or running before you check the hard disk.
2. Click Go in the Finder menu and select Utilities.
3. Click the First Aid tab to display that window.

4. Select your hard disk from the list on the left.

5. Click Verify Disk. You will see a warning that your Mac may be slow or unresponsive while the process takes place. Click the Verify Disk button in the warning window and wait while Disk Utility works.

6. If no errors are found on your hard disk, you'll see a message "The volume Macintosh HD appears to be OK" in green lettering at the bottom of the screen, as shown here:

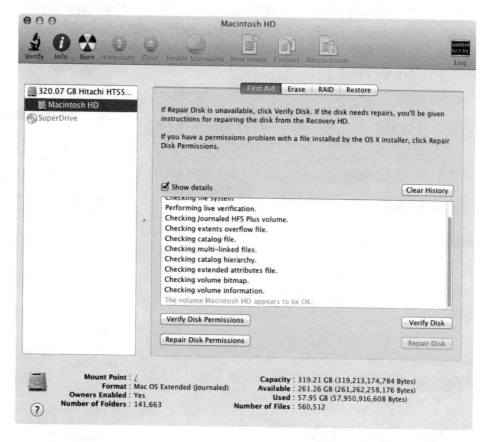

7. If errors were found on your hard disk, you'll need to repair them. In order to do this, you need to restart your Mac with another disk.

Delete Library Caches

Caches store information for your applications and help them run more effectively and quickly. However, if a cache file becomes corrupted, the application may crash or cause you grief in some other way. Most of your cache files are in the OS X Library, and deleting selected cache files can often solve problems with applications.

To troubleshoot a single application, delete the cache files associated with it to see if they were the cause of the problem.

1. Check to make sure the application you want to troubleshoot isn't open.
2. Find the cache file or folder associated with the application you're testing. You can get there by opening Finder, clicking Macintosh HD, and then clicking Library and opening the Caches folder.
3. Open the application again to see if it still has problems. If it does, you can drag the cache out of the trash and resume troubleshooting.

Fix Incorrect File Associations

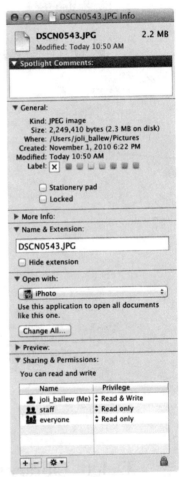

If your files open up in the wrong programs, there may be a problem with the default file associations on your Mac, or the file extension may be corrupted in some way. Let's say you have just installed Photoshop Elements 10. You accept the defaults during installation, and now, all of the JPEGS open up in PE10, even though you really prefer to view JPEGS in another program. To change the file association, do the following:

1. Locate the file you want to change in Finder and click it once to highlight it.
2. Choose File | Get Info (or use COMMAND-I).
3. Click Open With and select the application, as shown here.

Note You can also change all of the file associations for a file type by clicking the Change All button.

Use Recovery HD

A clever and incredibly useful new addition that came with Lion OS X is the Recovery HD. When either Lion or Mountain Lion was first installed on your Mac, OS X created a hidden partition on your hard drive that can be used as a separate volume to boot in case of emergency (for example, if you have problems with your regular hard drive that prevent it from functioning properly). This "secret" drive is called Recovery HD. It contains a number of utilities to fix your ailing hard drive, restore files, and reinstall OS X if needed. Prior to Lion, you had to locate your Mac's OS X installation disc and boot from that in order to repair disk errors or reinstall OS X if you needed to. In this next section we'll look at how to use Recovery HD to repair disk errors, restore from a Time Machine backup, and reinstall OS X.

Use Recovery HD to Repair Disk Errors

If your hard drive is causing you problems or you found errors on it when you checked it with Disk Utility, you can use Recovery HD to repair your hard drive. As you learned in the last section, you can diagnose disk errors with Disk Utility, but you need a separate startup drive to repair them. Recovery HD is just such a drive. To repair disk errors:

1. Hold down COMMAND-R while your Mac is starting up. You can either restart your Mac or hold the keys down when you turn your computer on.
2. Release the keys when you see the Apple logo.
3. When Recovery HD has completed starting up, you should see a OS X Utilities window (as shown in Figure 14-3).
4. Select Disk Utility, and then click Continue.
5. Select the disk you want to repair from the list on the left.
6. Click Repair Disk.

Note   If your Mac doesn't have a Recovery HD, you can use Internet Recovery to run OS X Utilities to repair your disk.

Not every Mac will have the Recovery HD. You must be running Lion or later. If you don't have the Recovery HD because you have an older operating system or for some other reason, you can repair disk errors by using the installation disc that came with your Mac when you first bought it or by using Internet Recovery with Lion or Mountain Lion (explained later in this chapter).

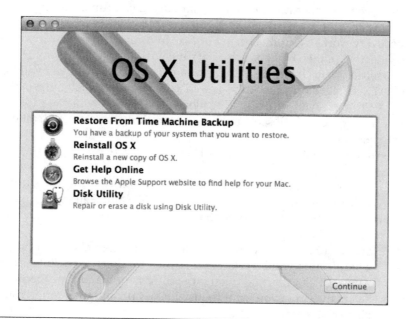

FIGURE 14-3   OS X Utilities in Recovery HD

Restore from Time Machine Backup

If you are having serious problems getting your Mac to function, you can restore your entire operating system from a Time Machine backup, including all your data, applications, user accounts, and settings. You must have a complete Time Machine backup that contains all your system files.

 Restoring from a Time Machine backup erases *everything* from the existing drive and replaces it with your last complete Time Machine backup.

To restore from a Time Machine backup:

1. Restart your Mac and press COMMAND-R to get to the OS X Utilities window in Recovery HD.
2. Select Restore From Time Machine Backup, and then click Continue.
3. Select the Time Machine drive and then the specific backup you want to restore from.
4. Choose the drive you want to erase. You should see another warning about the fact that you are about to erase the existing drive. Click Continue to proceed with the process. It may take an hour or more for the original disk to be erased and replaced with the backup.

Reinstall OS X with Internet Recovery

When you've tried other ways to revive your Mac and are still confronted with an ailing computer (or nonfunctioning hard disk), you can reinstall OS X with Internet Recovery. This is a good option if you don't have Recovery HD on your Mac. Internet Recovery works by connecting your Mac to Apple's servers over your Internet connection (either Wi-Fi or Ethernet) and downloading Recovery HD. Once you download the Recovery disk image, you boot from that and you will have a new copy of OS X installed on your Mac—as well as having access to all the other options in OS X Utilities. Even with a fast broadband connection, you can expect the process to take a long time. You'll see a progress bar tracking the estimated amount of time to complete the download.

To reinstall OS X with Internet Recovery:

1. Restart your Mac and press COMMAND-R when you hear the startup chimes. Release the keys when you see a prompt asking you to select a network.
2. Select a network and type the password. You should see the OS X Utilities window in Recovery HD.
3. Select Reinstall OS X and press RETURN, and then click Continue. You should see a verification window stating that your computer's eligibility is being verified by Apple. Click Continue to send the information and start the installation process.
4. Select the drive you want to install OS X on and then enter your Apple ID and password when prompted.

Note   OS X Internet Recovery is available on all Macs that came with Lion or Mountain Lion (mid-2011 or later). However, if you have a Mac that you bought prior to 2011, you may still be able to use Internet Recovery with a firmware upgrade from Apple. See Apple's support page to see if your computer is eligible: http://support .apple.com/kb/HT4904.

Use Target Disk Mode to Remove Files from a Problem Mac

If you can't get your Mac to boot to Recovery or find that it won't boot at all, you can recover files you need from your ailing Mac using Target Disk Mode. Target Disk Mode is built into Macs that have a FireWire or Thunderbolt port, and it allows you to use one Mac (in this case, a sick one) as an external hard drive when it's connected to a healthy computer. You can then move important data from the target disk to a functioning Mac.

In order to use this mode you'll need another Mac and either a FireWire cable or Thunderbolt cable. Thunderbolt ports are included on most Mac models after 2011. If you have an earlier Mac, you may have ports that support a FireWire cable. You can identify a FireWire port by looking for a symbol shaped like a Y with a circle in the middle. A Thunderbolt port will have a small thunderbolt symbol next to it. You can purchase either cable at Apple's online store. Once you have a spare Mac and a cable at your disposal, do the following to salvage files from your ailing Mac:

1. Connect your problem Mac to a host Mac using either a FireWire cable or Thunderbolt cable.
2. Restart your problem Mac and hold and press the T key. If you do this correctly, you should see either a FireWire symbol (it looks like a Y) or a Thunderbolt symbol on the screen of your problem Mac. Alternatively, you can boot to Target Disk Mode by clicking System Preferences and selecting Startup Disk, and then clicking the Target Disk Mode button. Click Restart when prompted and wait for the Mac to reboot.
3. On the screen of the host Mac, you should see your problem Mac's hard drive appear as an external drive on the desktop.
4. Double-click the hard drive and copy your files to your host Mac.
5. Drag the problem Mac's hard drive to Trash and press the EJECT key to remove it.

You won't be able to use Target Disk Mode if you set a firmware password for your Mac (as discussed in Chapter 13). If you have FileVault enabled, you'll need the FileVault password to access the home folder of your problem Mac on the host Mac.

If you have one Mac with a FireWire port and another with a Thunderbolt port, you can still access Target Disk Mode by using an adapter. You can also connect a FireWire 800 to a FireWire 400 device (each have a different number of pins) using a converter cable. Both are available at the Apple store.

Index